PRESENTS

Al Schmitt on Vocal and Instrumental Recording Technique

Al Schmitt on Vocal and Instrumental Recording Technique

AL SCHMITT
Adaptation by BILL GIBSON

BASED ON THE AUDIOVISUAL COURSES
METALLIANCE ACADEMY PRESENTS:
AL SCHMITT ON USING MICROPHONES AND
METALLIANCE ACADEMY PRESENTS:
AL SCHMITT ON RECORDING VOCAL SESSIONS
AVAILABLE ON GROOVE3.COM

Hal Leonard Books
An Imprint of Hal Leonard LLC

Published in 2018 by Hal Leonard Books
An Imprint of Hal Leonard LLC
7777 West Bluemound Road
Milwaukee, WI 53213

Trade Book Division Editorial Offices
33 Plymouth St., Montclair, NJ 07042

CREDITS

Grateful acknowledgment is made to the following individuals and companies whose product images and photographs may appear in this book:

AMS/Neve; Audio-Technica; Avid; Brauner Microphones; Stanley Coutant, www.coutant.org; Electro-Voice; Georg Neumann GmbH; GML, LLC; Harman; Maag Audio; Martinsound; Royer Labs Microphones; Shure; Sony Music Entertainment; Summit Audio; RCA; TELEFUNKEN Elektroakustik; Tube-Tech; Universal Audio

Printed in the United States of America
Book design by Kristina Rolander

Library of Congress Cataloging-in-Publication Data

Names: Schmitt, Al, author. | Gibson, Bill (William A.)
Title: Al Schmitt on vocal and instrumental recording techniques / Al Schmitt; adaptation by Bill Gibson.
Description: Montclair, NJ : Hal Leonard Books, 2018. | "METAlliance Academy Presents."
Identifiers: LCCN 2018014518 | ISBN 9781495094514
Subjects: LCSH: Sound recordings--Production and direction. | Popular music--Production and direction.
Classification: LCC ML3790 .S293 2018 | DDC 781.49--dc23
LC record available at https://lccn.loc.gov/2018014518

www.halleonardbooks.com

Contents

1. VOCAL MIC CHOICE 1
First Playback with Musicians in the Control Room 2
Choosing the Vocal Mic 3

2. VOCALIST, STYLE, AND LEAKAGE 7
Microphone Technique 9
Getting to Know the Artist 10

3. THE RECORDING SPACE 11
Sight Lines 11
Setting the Mics to Omni 14

4. SETTING UP THE BAND 15
Unfamiliar Instruments 16
Making Them Happy 16
Miking a Male Vocalist 18
Miking a Female Vocalist 19
Miking Background Vocalists 20
Miking a Choir 20
Duets 21
Choosing a Preamp for Vocals 21

5. RECORDING THE RHYTHM SECTION 25
Recording Drums 25
Acoustic Bass 30
Electric Bass 33
Piano 34
Upright Piano 34
Harpsichord 35
Acoustic Guitar 35
Electric Guitar 36

6. RECORDING WOODWINDS, BRASS, AND STRINGS 37
Saxophone 37
Brass 39
Strings 41

7. AL'S TOOL CHEST 43
Microphones 43
Preamps and EQs 99
Compressors 106

Conclusion 109
About the Author 111

Al Schmitt on Vocal and Instrumental Recording Technique

1

Vocal Mic Choice

Before we even go into the studio, I interact with the producer to find out what he or she is looking for, the type of sound, and what the instrumentation is. The more information I have, the better prepared I am when the session comes around. So hopefully, when the musicians come to the studio, there's not a lot that has to be changed. The drummer might ask me to lower the overhead mics a little to get more of his cymbals, or we might need to address a couple other small issues, but if we've done our homework, and we're ready to go when the musicians arrive, everybody wins.

On some occasions, the rundown (the first time through the song to test balances and levels) is the take we use for the record—this has happened quite a few times, actually. We might end up recording six or seven takes and then somebody will say, "Let's go back to that first take," and that first take is the one with all the magic. It may not be perfect, but it's got all that spontaneity and the stuff that makes great music. When we recorded George Benson's *Breezin'*, six of the eight songs we recorded were all first takes. Only six songs went on the album—all six of the first takes! That was with the whole rhythm section, and percussion, and everything! It was just unbelievable.

FIRST PLAYBACK WITH MUSICIANS IN THE CONTROL ROOM

Normally, we'll record a first take so all the musicians can come into the control room and hear how everything is working together. Some engineers switch to the big speakers and crank the volume up when the musicians come into the control room so everything will sound more impressive. I don't do that because I love the sound of my monitors. I might turn the volume up a little so they can hear what I'm hearing, but I've never monitored at high levels. When I was recording more rock 'n' roll, and the bands wanted to listen to the playback really loud, I would show them where the volume knob was, tell them to listen as loud as they wanted, and I'd leave the room until they were done listening.

When the musicians hear the take, they'll adjust their parts on their own. But I talk to them and find if they're happy with the sounds. I'll ask if they have enough echo and if the earphone balance is okay. And then I make sure the drummer and the bass player are happy. I try to get all the things out of the way that would make me a little uncomfortable if I were playing. Once I know they're as comfortable as possible, I might direct them to lean in to the mic on certain sections, or maybe back off on other sections. That way they'll do a little of the self-limiting. A little mic technique can go a long way.

Nine times out of ten everything is cool. They might say they're happy with the sound, or maybe it's a little too bright, or maybe the sound isn't bright enough. I'm very accommodating, and really try to give the musicians whatever they need to be completely comfortable so they can deliver a great performance. I'll just say, "Ok, we'll fix that," and I'll change the mic, or whatever it takes to help the musicians relax and perform—I always have options ready to go. Since I use a lot of tube mics, I have extras plugged in and warmed up so they'll be ready to rotate in if we need them. Tube mics can take several minutes to warm up to the point where they can sound their best. We keep extras plugged in so we can quickly make a change.

I'm always talking with the producer and getting his or her feedback. During the first take, I'm either getting their approval, or I might be asked something like, "Can I get a little tighter sound on this section?" Or, "I'd like a little more open sound on the B section." We make those adjustments and go on to take two.

I used to get very nervous when the players would come into the control room to listen. I remember when I did my first large orchestra date in New York, and I was standing in back while everybody listened to the take. I had my hands in my pockets because I was shaking so much. When the playback finished, I walked up to the board, sat down, took my hands out, and grabbed on—we had rotary faders then. I grabbed onto the faders so they couldn't see how much I was shaking. I was so nervous. Also, I was deathly afraid of French horns. I used to dream about French horns and how they would be everywhere haunting me. I don't get nervous anymore. I'm past that stage, thank God.

CHOOSING THE VOCAL MIC

There's a lot that goes into choosing a mic for a vocal session, but the first thing I think about is the type of music. It makes a difference whether there's a male or a female singer. If we're going to do vocals live in the same room with the rest of the musicians, I'll approach it differently than if we need total isolation on the vocal track. I might put the singer in a vocal booth to get as much separation as we can. If I'm going to overdub the vocalist later, I want to make sure that the mic we use in the initial session will also be a great mic for overdubs—I need to choose the mic that will sound best in both situations. This is an important consideration if there's a chance we're going to use the reference tracks in the mix along with the overdubs. And it matters who the manager is, and how easy he or she is to get along with.

For vocals, my initial "go-to" microphone is the Neumann U 47. That's my favorite vocal mic, and it's the right choice about 90 percent of the time. On female vocalists, I might use something else. I have a Brauner VM1 microphone that I like a lot. The Audio-Technica AT5040 is a great mic on female vocals. When I start a session for an artist, I'll have two to three microphones set up ready to go, and we'll check them out quickly. Sometimes the microphone you think will be the least likely to sound best is the one you use. You have to use your ears and pick the mic that sounds best.

The Neumann U 47 is my go-to mic for vocals.

(FROM GEORG NEUMANN GMBH)

The Brauner VM1

The Audio-Technica 5040

I was doing the *Breezin'* album with George Benson, and we had everybody in the same room—all sitting around the drummer. George was right there just sitting and playing. All the songs were instrumentals except one: "This Masquerade." When it came time to do the vocal, I hadn't planned on it, and I wasn't really ready. They said, "Okay, we're going do the vocal tune now." I figured that since he's sitting right in the middle of the room, and the drums are right in the middle of everything, we'd overdub the vocal later. So I looked around and grabbed the first mic on a stand I found. It was an Electro-Voice 666—you could hammer nails with that mic! I just stuck it in front of George figuring, well, we'll get it when we do overdubs.

He killed the vocal! That was it; that's what we used. One take! When we were starting the next album I did with George, I had a beautiful Neumann U 47 set up for his vocals, and he said, "No, no! I want to use that little black mic. You know, that little mic we used last time." It took me a while, but I eventually talked him into using the U 47. It just goes to show that it's the performance that really counts. If you capture a great performance, even on a bad microphone, it'll work because it's the emotion of the performance that sells the record—that's what happened with "This Masquerade." That record sounds great on the radio, and we just used that cheap microphone.

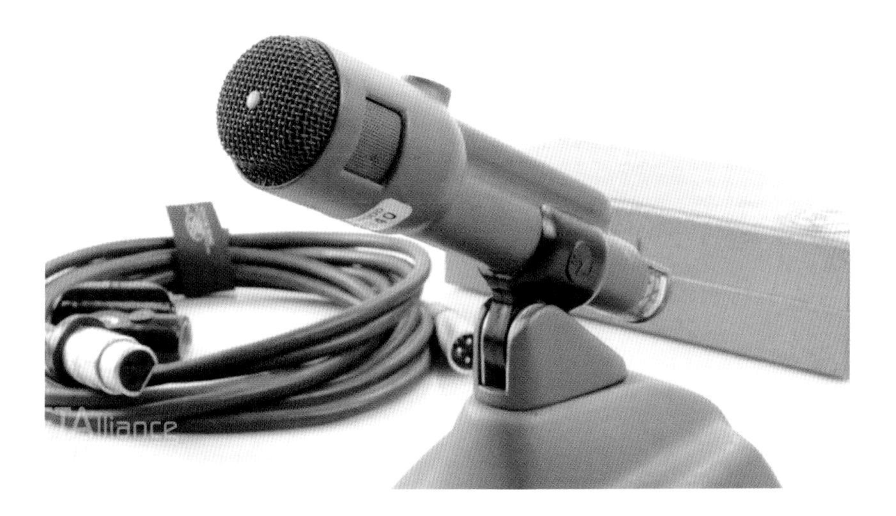

We recorded "This Masquerade," and I wasn't really ready. So I looked around and grabbed the first mic on a stand I found. It was an EV 666—you could hammer nails with that mic! I just stuck it in front of George figuring, well, we'll get it when we do overdubs. He killed the vocal! That was it; that's what we used. One take! (ELECTRO-VOICE)

When I'm recording a new artist, I'll try different mics and two or three different preamps, until I find the sound that works best for the music. I have a Martech MSS-10 preamp that I use. I have Neve preamps and Studer valve preamps. I'll try different things until I find the right sound. If I hear a demo or something an artist has previously recorded, I can get an insight into the texture of the voice—that helps a lot when I'm choosing which mic and preamp to use.

Martinsound Martech
MSS-10 preamp

Neve 1073 and 1081Classic preamp

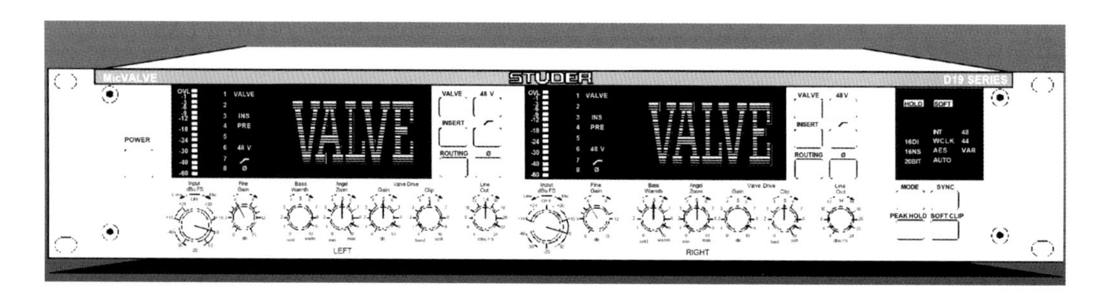

Studer D19 MicVALVE preamp

2

Vocalist, Style, and Leakage

I've worked with a lot of different musicians, rooms, genres, and types of artists. And even though a session one day might be very different from a session on another, that doesn't mean I'll necessarily change what I do or how I do it. I normally reach first for my go-to microphones because I'm familiar with how they'll perform in most recording scenarios. Of course, there are exceptions, such as when I'm recording an opera singer, or a classical record. Then I might use two microphones on the singer, with one maybe a foot and a half from the singer in front, and then a separate mic maybe two and a half feet away, but up a little higher to catch some of the room ambiance. That way, when the vocalist goes from a whisper to a roar, we can capture it all without distortion. However, normally it doesn't matter. If it's a rock 'n' roll date, I'll still try to use my same microphones. I set up the drums the same. The only difference would be in setting up mics on the piano. If I'm recording a classical piano, I certainly would mic it differently than I would on a pop or rock date.

Getting back to vocal mics, once I've settled in and I've made my choices of the preamp and microphone, I like to use the Fairchild compressor on vocals—I'll just tap it so there's no more than a dB or two of gain reduction. I use it basically to just get the Fairchild sound. It does something to the vocal that's really pleasant.

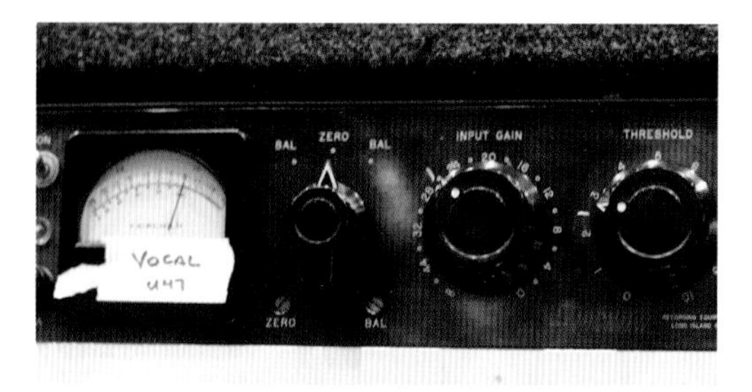

Fairchild 660 (mono)

If I'm doing a rock session, and the artist wants to be in the room with the band—and we're getting all kinds of leakage—I'll try a microphone that has a narrower polar pattern—often a solid-state condenser microphone rather than the tube mic. When I was working with Sam Cooke, he was usually in the room with the rest of the band. I used a U 47 on him all the time. The only reason to make a change would be if I was unhappy with the way the vocal was hitting the microphone. There are so many great microphones. I would always be willing to try a Neumann M 49. Neumann microphones are great. The Telefunken 251 is a great microphone. Sometimes you'll find a minor difference between a U 47 and a 251, but if the artist prefers one over the other, that's the way you should go. The most important thing is keeping the artist happy, which is all about capturing the best possible performance. It's just like George Benson recording on an Electro-Voice 666 dynamic mic—it's the performance that matters. If you don't have anything else but an SM57, you can still capture a great performance—that's what counts.

Telefunken 251

Sometimes an artist or a producer might want to do something a certain way to match a sound they liked or heard in another recording, even from a different era. For example, when I started recording big bands years ago, the drummer was always in the room with the brass, and we always set the drums up right next to the trumpets—always! That was the ideal spot for them because the trumpets wanted to hear the drums—that was before earphones became important in the studio. If the artist wants that kind of a sound, like having the drums out in the open with rest of a big band, you have to go for it. You need to find the right spot for the drums, and you'll probably want to position baffles around the kit so the drums are isolated a bit. If the band members are all wearing headphones, it's a little easier to do that. On the early recordings, when nobody was using headphones, we had to set the band up the way they felt most comfortable, and only then would we work with mic position to get the best sound.

I don't change my microphone setup whether the drummer is in a booth, or out in the room with the rest of the band. If we're overdubbing drums, which happens, I might put some room mics up to capture the ambient sound of the drums in the room, but that's not typical for me.

Again, once everything has settled in with the setup, and everyone is ready to go, I like to record a take. Then I ask everybody to come into the control room to listen to the take. I want to make sure the artist is happy with the sound, that everyone is comfortable, and that the earphone mixes are good. Once that's established, then we can really focus on getting a great performance.

MICROPHONE TECHNIQUE

Even today, I always ride the record level when I'm recording a vocalist. We didn't have compressors back when I learned to record vocals so I'd have to learn the song quickly and help out by boosting the quiet spots. On the loud spots, I'd bring the level back. Vocalists like Rosemary Clooney had excellent microphone technique. With her, you could set the fader and forget it because she leaned into the mic when she needed to, she backed off when she'd get loud, or she'd sing over the mic if there was a plosive that might pop. Mic technique is kind of a lost art now, so, as the engineer, you have to control all of the levels, make sure the singer is always heard, and you need to make sure that there are no problems with popping plosives. You need to learn the song as quickly as possible, and you need to know when the vocalist is going to belt out so you can back the fader down. I'll ask the artist to just back off a little bit at that point and maybe sing a little over the microphone. It's all teamwork. Everybody is working for the same thing—to get the best out of the artist.

GETTING TO KNOW THE ARTIST

When I start a new project, I talk to the producer and find out the instrumentation, the arranger, and definitely who the artist is. If it's an artist I've worked with before, then I know what to do. If not, we'll talk about how to work together and whether the artist is very nervous, or if it's their first recording session—sometimes you have to pamper them to make it work. I tell them how far to stand from the mic, and that if they're going to have loud points in the song, to raise their head a little to aim over the microphone. I don't want to give them too much to think about because they should be thinking about the performance. Once we get a chance to do a rundown of the song with the vocalist on the mic, I'll ask the producer what he thinks. If he likes the sound, great. Or, he might think it's too sibilant or not bright enough. If it's not right, we'll try another approach. As an engineer, your name goes on the back of the record too, but keeping the artist happy is the most important part. The artist is first, and then the producer. They are the ones you need to make happy. Sometimes they might want something you wouldn't do on your own, but if that's what makes them the most comfortable, you should go along with it. Always do your best to keep the artist happy and comfortable.

If I'm going to do a vocal session with an artist who has been around for a while, but I've never worked with them, I'll listen to records they've done. I'll listen and see what they did previously, and hopefully I can do as well or better. I also talk to other engineers. I ask, "Hey Ed, what do I look for with this artist? What do I have to watch out for?" We all help one another that way. Some artists have terrible reputations, but when you ask around, their reputation is a lot worse than they really are—they're really pussycats in the studio. On the other hand, some artists you'd expect to be a walk in the park can be a bit more on the other end of things. They want a little more of this, or a little more of that—they're just not comfortable.

3

The Recording Space

The first thing I think about when I'm recording is the room—what I might already know about it, and how we're going to set up. The way we set up in the space is the most important thing in the world because it affects how the musicians feel in the room and how they can communicate.

SIGHT LINES

Everybody needs a clear line of vision and they need to be able to hear what they need to hear. When headphones weren't commonly used, the setup was very crucial, but even today we still need to make sure everything is just right for the musicians. I recently did a project with an artist, and we did everything live with no earphones. Everybody set up around the artist and it turned out great.

The first thing I think about when I'm recording is the room.

It's also very important to make sure everything is working and checked out before the artist arrives. It's no good when an artist shows up and has to stand around while everything gets set up.

As engineers, we don't always have a choice of where we're going to record. If there's an appropriately sized vocal booth, I'll use that, but I always check the sound in the booth to make sure I'm happy with it. If not, I'd rather have the vocalist out in the room, surrounded by gobos, and deal with the leakage from the rest of the musicians. But, whenever possible, I try to keep as much separation as possible in case we need to fix some things or record overdubs later.

I've worked often at Avatar in Manhattan (now Power Station at BerkleeNYC). Their vocal booth is really tiny, but acoustically it just sounds great. You wouldn't think a room so small would sound that good, but it does. Vocals recorded in that booth have a lot of presence and a nice quality.

Every room has a different sound. Capitol's studio A has a sound. Capitol B has another sound. As an engineer, you work the room as best you can and get the best possible sounds out of it. If I'm working in a room for the first time, I always try to talk to somebody that's worked there. I'll call another engineer or producer and ask him or her what to look out for. I'll talk to other people and find out who the best assistant is to help me along with the room. A good assistant will tell me the live and dead spots in the room. It's important to have someone who knows the room and has a history with finding the best-sounding parts of the studio.

Sometimes I build a vocal booth using gobos out in the room with the rhythm section. It usually works well because a really good singer can interact with the musicians and that's important. Dealing with space is a matter of adjusting to your environment. Whatever space you have, you need to make it sound great, and you need to work on it until you find the answer.

Some singers have trouble with headphones and want to sing in the control room. Before I used headphones, singers would do that all the time. Some vocalists sing in the control room, sitting on the couch in the back with the speakers blaring, holding a mic. If that's what they want, I do my best to make them comfortable. You have to be willing to compromise and work with what you have.

I compromise on microphones, especially if I'm working with somebody who wants to sing in the control room. I'll do whatever it takes to get the performance from the artist, and to get the right performance. It's all about the artist's performance, and the emotion in the recording. People don't buy records because they like the way the snare drum sounds. They buy records because it touches them somewhere emotionally—that's what I try to capture. And if I have to use an old crystal microphone to accomplish that, that's what it'll be. We have to sometimes swallow our own pride even though we know we can get a better sound on a vocal. We need to deal with the sound we have—that's what we capture. In a space that sounds lousy, you just do the best you can. Sometimes you can brighten it up a little with the live side of some gobos, depending on what microphones you use, where you place the microphone, and how you position the artist.

If you're in very live room, you might need to deaden it somewhat. I put blankets up on the walls sometimes to deaden a room. Engineers aren't always blessed to have the perfect studio, perfect control room, or perfect musicians. Sometimes it's a scuffle. It takes a lot of knowledge, and a lot of experience to work in so many different places. That's why the better engineers keep working.

SETTING THE MICS TO OMNI

I record a lot differently than many people because I set most of my microphones to the omni position. I love the sound of things leaking back and forth between the mics. It makes everything sound bigger, and it produces more depth. But there's good leakage and bad leakage. If you're using good microphones, and you're in a room that sounds good, that will help the final product sound bigger and better.

In a room that sounds good, setting the mics to omni makes everything sound bigger, and it produces more depth.

If you're using SM57s, and mics that are designed to be closer to the source, the leakage won't sound good. If you're in a bad-sounding room, your hands are tied, and you need to move the mics closer and set them to cardioid just to decrease the negative effect of the room sound. But I really prefer to embrace the leakage in a great-sounding room and open up the mics to omni, so I can get a bigger sound.

4

Setting Up the Band

The way I set up a band depends on what studio I'm recording in. Whether it's Capitol in Los Angeles, Power Station at BerkleeNYC in New York, or anywhere else, the first step is to make sure I'm prepared for the setup. In advance, I check out the studio's microphone list so I know what I have to bring of my own. I go over the floor plan, confirm how many vocal booths they have, and whether or not they have a drum booth. Once I figure out a setup, my assistant and I will go over it together and make sure we're ready to go.

When we're setting up for large sessions, we pretty much use the same microphones each time. We'll use the same microphones on the trumpets, the same on trombones, and the same on saxes. I have my mics that I use on the piano and the upright bass and the drums. I try to make it as comfortable as possible for the musicians by not having too many microphones right in their faces. I'd rather have the mics set so that the musicians are very comfortable and aren't consciously focused on the fact that there are mics nearby.

UNFAMILIAR INSTRUMENTS

If perhaps we're recording an instrument I have never seen before—and that's pretty rare at this point—I'll go out into the studio and talk to the musician about where the sound comes from the instrument. And I'll ask if he or she has recorded before, and where the mic was positioned. And they'll usually share that, "Yeah, they put the microphone here and that worked the last time." If you do that, then at least you have a starting point. As a young engineer, the musicians in the room are your best friends. Make sure they're comfortable. And make sure they have a chance to hear what you're hearing in the control room. Most good musicians are able to make quick adjustments that will make everything sound better once they hear the recording playback. I try to play back everything after the first take and bring everybody in so they can hear exactly what they're doing and how everything is fitting together. They'll make adjustments while you're making adjustments. Take two is usually so much better than take one.

MAKING THEM HAPPY

If the musicians are comfortable, and not thinking about the temperature, or any other comfort concerns, they can just concentrate on doing their vocal, and you're going to get their best performance. Our job as engineers is to make sure they're comfortable—that there's water, and Kleenex, and that the earphones are set up correctly and well balanced. I try to make sure we've addressed all of those issues at the front end of the session so everything runs smoothly. You don't want the artist thinking about anything else but the performance.

We'll do whatever it takes to make the artist comfortable in the studio. Years ago, I recorded Neil Young's album, *On the Beach*. We set up the studio at Sunset Sound like a living room. We had couches and lamps and everybody was sitting around like they were in somebody's living room playing and singing.

When we were recording Sinatra, he had Capitol build this special booth with air conditioning. We had a bottle of Jack Daniel's, we had Tootsie Rolls, which were his favorite thing—he loved those. We had Camel cigarettes, and we were set. Phil Ramone was producing, and I was engineering.

When Frank came in, he said, "Where do you want me?"

I said, "I think you're going to be in there."

He said, "I'm not going in there."

I said, "Where do you want to be?"

And he said, "How about right here."

He was right in front of the brass section! I said, "Okay," and went back to the control room. I looked at Phil who had turned white! We had thought we would be able to isolate Frank's vocal to a separate track so we'd have all kinds of flexibility and options later in the process. So Phil and I are in the control room for the first rundown, and the band is cookin'. We had two days with the band before Frank showed up, so we had all the balances set and we knew tempos and everything. He stood right in front of the brass section—right in front of the trombones and trumpets. He opened his mouth and this gorgeous sound came out and I looked at Phil and he had this shit-eatin' grin on his face. Frank's manager and Phil and I all had goosebumps it sounded so great. I had never worked with Frank before, and he was my idol. It was the thrill of a lifetime. Sometimes your best laid plans don't work out, but if you can keep making the artist comfortable throughout the recording process, something else might happen to make it even better.

We wound up using a wireless microphone on Frank because that's what made him comfortable. Frank didn't want to go into the booth he had requested and that we had stocked with some of his favorite things. He wanted to be right in front of the brass, and that's what we had to deal with. That's the problem we had to solve.

I like to be as prepared as I can with the artist's cue mix. The approach we take depends on whether we're doing a vocal overdub to existing tracks, a big orchestra session, or a rhythm section with a vocalist. If we're recording overdubs to existing tracks, then I certainly want to get out in front of that before the artist shows up. We'll make sure the headphones are getting a really good balance with the right amount of echo on things, and that the headphone mix is in a great place. That way, when the artist comes in, we'll already have a nice mix set up for them. They can make it louder or softer if they want, and we'll set up an echo feed for their mixer so they can adjust the reverb. We'll do whatever we can to make sure they're perfectly comfortable.

If we're doing a big orchestra date, or a rhythm section and a vocalist, 90 percent of the time my assistant sets the headphone mixes for the artist and the producer, while I'm getting my balances together, making sure the mics are in the right place, and verifying that everything is working. He'll also make sure the headphones are adjusted when the musicians make requests for a little more of this or a little less of that.

Most studios now have a good system for getting a good mix on headphones. In most cases, the musicians have their own small mixer. We set up a few different feeds so they can fine-tune their own mix. We tend to supply the rhythm section on one feed, maybe brass on another, a solo on another, and then the vocal and vocal echo. They can control their own mix to find a balance that makes them comfortable. Sometimes we'll go out and put the earphones on to hear what the artist is hearing. We might not be able to figure out how they could even sing to it, the mix is so off, but if that's what they like, and that's what makes them comfortable, then that's what's going to help them give their best performance.

I try to make them as comfortable as possible, but sometimes you run into a rare situation where the artist doesn't want to touch anything. So you have to make sure everything is comfortable. I always ask, "Are you happy with the phones? Do you hear enough voice? Do you have enough echo? Are you hearing the rhythm section?" I'll do anything I can to make it better.

MIKING A MALE VOCALIST

My first-choice go-to microphone for a male vocalist is the Neumann U 47. I remember when that mic first came out. They were 300 bucks. I should have bought a ton of them, but I didn't have 300 bucks back then. I also love the Telefunken 251. I think that's a great mic on a male vocal. Back in the old days, we used the RCA 77-DX. It was a ribbon mic, and this was before we had windscreens. We used to tape a pencil in front of the ribbon to redirect the air, which would get rid of plosive problems. The original AKG C12 is a great vocal mic, too.

In the old days, we sometimes used the RCA 77-DX on vocals

(PHOTO BY STANLEY COUTANT)

I rarely ever use dynamic mics on the vocal. At least, I try to stay away from them. If the artist really wanted to use a dynamic mic, I would, but I haven't had to use one in a long time.

MIKING A FEMALE VOCALIST

Sometimes I use the Audio-Technica AT5040. It's a great microphone for a female voice. I like the Telefunken 251, too. And some women sound great on a U 47. I usually have two or three microphones set up and ready to go when the singer arrives. I'll try one, and if I don't like it right away—I'll know whether it works or not as soon as I hear the voice on it—I'll just get rid of that one, we'll re-patch so the next mic is in the same signal chain, and we'll try that one. I always find something that works really well. The Audio-Technica AT5047 is an excellent vocal mic. I found it when Steve Genewick and I were in France teaching a seminar. Audio-Technica had sent it to the studio so we could test it out. We plugged the mic in to try it on a male vocalist and as soon I opened the mic, I looked at Steve and he looked me and we were both amazed at how great it sounded, and everyone in the room agreed. We didn't even try another mic because the 5047 just sounded fantastic.

Audio-Technica sent us the AT5047 to try while we were teaching a seminar in France. It's amazing!

MIKING BACKGROUND VOCALISTS

Years ago, I used an RCA 44 and put two singers on one side and two on the other, and it was great. It captured a great blend. We'd ask one singer to step forward a little and maybe have one step back, and we'd build the blend that way. The singers would basically blend themselves. That always worked well.

Today I'm using U 47s. If there are four singers, I'll put two mics up—one mic for two singers, and one mic for the other two. If it's a group where everyone is a lead singer, then it's different. Then I'll probably have one mic for each person. Take Six is a good example of that kind of vocal group. With them, they'll sing together, and when each guy gets a good take, he'll sit down and we'll run it again. Then the other guys do their parts until everybody's sitting. Once they're all sitting, you know you've got the full take.

I love the Neumann M 49. That's another great vocal mic and a great mic for backgrounds. I set it to bidirectional and put two singers on each side. A U 48, set the same way, is great for background vocals, too.

A lot of people don't know about the U 48, and a lot of photos of a Neumann U 47 might actually be a U 48. They're essentially the same mic, but the U 47 has cardioid and omnidirectional patterns, whereas the U 48 has cardioid and bidirectional patterns. So for background vocals, the U 48 would be a great choice set to bidirectional for two singers (one on each side of the mic), or four singers (two on each side of the mic).

MIKING A CHOIR

The last choir I worked on was with Neil Young, and we were at Sony Scoring Stage. We had 100 pieces—a 65 piece orchestra, and a 35 piece choir. I had four Neumann M 149s up on the choir. I had them two and two, split out in front of the choir. They sounded just great. It was fabulous. They were about ten feet in front of the choir and eight to ten feet high.

Sony Scoring Stage is one of the most beautiful sounding rooms in the world. I mean, it's like cream coming out of the speakers—it's just beautiful. Sometimes with choirs, I'll stack them on risers, with some on the floor, some on the small riser, and some on a higher riser. If you can't get the M 149s, good ribbon mics work well for choir, too.

I know I'm talking about all these great microphones, and, in many cases, I realize that I'm probably giving this information to many people who can't afford them. Just use the best mics you have and work with those. But I always recommend that people save their money when they can, and buy one really good mic instead of buying a lot of cheap mics. You'd be surprised how if you save to buy a great mic, and then save to buy another, and if you do that again, after a little while you'll build up a very nice microphone collection, and pretty soon you'll have a nice little arsenal of mics. But if you just keep buying a lot of cheap mics, all you'll end up with is a big box of inferior mics that don't sound good.

DUETS

I recorded a lot of the Sinatra duets, and I've recorded a lot of other duets with various artists. When both artists sing at the same time, I use two mics. And I try to keep them so they're close together, and I make sure they have eye contact with one another. That way, if they can see each another, they can sing off each other much more easily, and it's more likely they'll put more emotion into their performances.

I'd mic each singer in the same way I would if they were singing a solo. I'd choose from the same list of options, but there would be two mics in the same space instead of one. If I was recording a duet between a guy and a girl, I might use a U 47 on the guy, and an Audio-Technica 5040 on the girl. It's important to keep the singers close together because it ends up sounding like a natural duet. So many duets today are done where one person sings their part in Los Angeles, and the other person could be in China singing their part. You can spend a lot of time just matching up the quality of the different rooms so you don't end up with one real close kind of sound to one big bright open sound. You have to be conscious of that. Just be aware. Use your ears and some good sense to solve the problem.

CHOOSING A PREAMP FOR VOCALS

The preamps on the Neve 88R console in Capitol Studio A are really good. I helped design those preamps. Robin from Neve would come in there, and we'd listen, I'd make suggestions, and then he'd go back and makes some changes. We went through that process until we were satisfied. They sound great.

The Neve 88R in Capitol's Studio A

I have certain preamps that I lean toward for female vocals, and others for guys. I have some Studer tube preamps, the D19 Series MicVALVE that I like to use on female vocals. They warm the sound up a tiny bit. I have the Neve 1081s and 1073s that I like to use on guy's vocals. The Martech MSS-10 works great on lead singers—that's a really nice preamp. I have a whole rack of different options. I'll try different things. If the Martech doesn't work, I'll quickly patch over to one of my Neve preamps, and if that doesn't work, I'll try one of my Studer tube preamps. Sooner or later, I'm gonna find the right combination, and I do it really fast so it doesn't drag the singer's energy down.

The most important thing in a preamp is the clarity and how it responds to the vocal characteristics. Each preamp responds differently to each different voice, so you need to find that perfect marriage. It's very rare that I have much trouble finding the best combination of mic and preamp, though. I'm trying different combinations all the time. I know what to expect from my gear, but I might use a vintage mic with a newer preamp, or vice versa. It's really all about using your ears. For me, there's a little bell in my head that goes off when I find the right sound. I know that's the sound I want right away when I hear it. It's the same when I'm using echo on a vocal or whatever. I use combinations of things to find the right blend, and once I find what I'm listening for, I'm happy. Use your ears and listen closely. That's the most important thing.

I always have alternate microphones and preamps standing by. A combination of one or the other is going to work, and I try them all as quickly as possible. If I know who the singer is, before the session I'll listen to what they've done previously so I can get an idea of what combination of mic and preamp might be best for them. I can get ahead of the game that way. One of the most important things, no matter what you're doing, is that you should always be prepared. Always be ready. When I first got in this business, I was told to always be there early. Always check out your microphones. Always make sure your gear is in perfect condition so that when the artist or the band comes in, all you have to do is worry about what's going on with them, not your gear. You don't want your gear falling apart when the first take is going down! Check everything out ahead of time. Check your phasing on your microphones. Confirm that everything is functioning perfectly. Be prepared.

5

Recording the Rhythm Section

When I first started, we might only have six or eight channels for the entire group, and they were being mixed to mono. It was a great way to learn because we had to figure out how to get the most out our microphones, the room, and the artist. The way we record has progressed over the years, but I still rely on a lot of the things I learned early on.

RECORDING DRUMS

Back in New York when I first started, we only had an eight-input board. You could only put up eight microphones, so no matter how big the group was, you couldn't add more than eight inputs. Therefore, we rarely ever used more than one microphone on the drums. We would always put one mic up, usually right over the drums.

One day I was doing a jazz trio record, and the drummer was a very famous drummer by the name of Tiny Kahn. He was a big heavy-set guy, and he said, "Hey kid. Put a mic on the kick." I was very young but I looked at him and said, "What, are you nuts?" And he said, "No, no, no, I'm telling you, put a mic on the kick and then just turn it up a little bit and see what it sounds like." This was in the early '50s. I was intimidated by him. He outweighed me by three times, and he was a very famous bebop drummer of his time, so I did what he asked. I had an RCA 44 ribbon microphone, so I dropped it down in front of the kick and about ten inches away. We had rotary faders, and I gently brought it in until I could hear it and stopped.

When we played back the first take, Tiny came in to listen and he said, "See, you learned something kid. That sounds really good." So he was happy, I was happy, and I did that whenever I could—whenever I wasn't already using all of the channels for other things. When I was recording small quartets or trios, I'd add a mic on the kick and it seemed to work out well. I think the moral to that story is: hey, if someone asks you to do something that you wouldn't normally do in the studio, give it a try. It just might work out great, and if it doesn't work, it doesn't work. You'll know right away.

The AKG D 12 E. I have the fourth AKG D12 ever made and it's my favorite kick drum mic. If I don't have it with me, an AKG D112 or the D 12 E work great, too.

- **SNARE DRUM.** On the snare, I use two mics. On top, I use an AKG 452 with the 10 dB pad engaged, positioned about 1 to 1½ inches above the rim, aiming at the spot on the head where the drummer's sticks strike. We sometimes adjust the mic a little farther in or out, depending on the drums and the player.

I use an SM57 under the drum, pointing up at the snares as much as possible. I put the 57 very close to the actual snares underneath the drum, and I set it out of phase on the console. When I'm blending the two mics, I get a sound I like with the top mic, and then I add just enough of the mic underneath to give the snare sound a nice crack—that snap that we all look for in a snare drum sound. You can easily adjust the sound just by bringing more or less of the 57 underneath. And if the drummer plays with brushes, I don't use the mic underneath because I don't need that crack. I try to get that warmth of the brushes from the top of the snare.

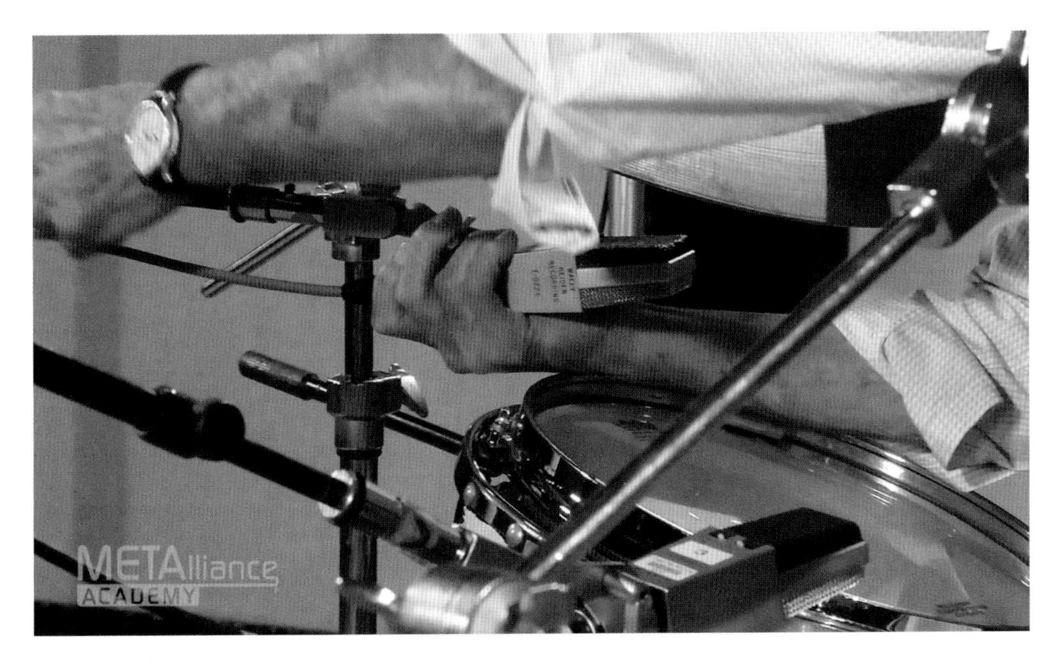

AKG C414s on the toms

- **HI-HAT.** On the hi-hat I use an AKG C452. I keep it about six to eight inches above the hi-hat, and I aim it toward the outer edge of the top cymbal, but away from where the air comes out when the cymbals come together. I position the mic on the other side of the hi-hat rod and clutch from the drummer so the mic is out of the drummer's way, and there's very little chance the drummer will hit the mic.
- **OVERHEADS.** Audio-Technica makes a great microphone called the AT5045 that I like to use on overheads now. The 5045 has a crystal-clear sound at the top end, and all the drummers love it. Another microphone that works very well for overheads

is the AKG C452. And the Royer stereo ribbon mic sounds great as an overhead. I also use a pair of AKG C12 VRs sometimes—they're beautiful microphones. If the drums are in a booth, or if they're in a room where I'm worried about a lot of other things leaking in, I'll definitely set the overheads to cardioid. But if I'm in an open room like Capitol A, I'll have them open all the way around in omni. I position the two overhead mics two or three feet above the drummer's head, aiming down toward the cymbals. When I start balancing in the room, I'll have the drummer or the drum tech play the kit, and I'll open the overheads first. The sound that we're capturing with the overheads is very important, so I'll raise or lower the mics until there is a good balance of the drums and cymbals. Once I've found the sound I want from the overheads, I open up the kick mic, and then work my way through the rest of the close mics. From that point, once the session starts we're in good shape, and might just need to fine tune things a bit and we're ready to go.

Audio-Technica AT5045

AKG C12 VR

If I'm doing a rock date, I might place a couple mics out in the room, eight to ten feet in front of the drums—or sometimes even farther away—to capture the sound of the drums in the room. In the mix, I can add as much of the room as I want, or if I don't end up needing the room, I'll mute those tracks. However, sometimes the sound of the room mics opens up the drum sound quite a bit.

I played drums when I was a kid, so I have an affinity for drummers. I'm friends with the drummers I work with regularly. They're all a little wacky, and we love that about them. With everything we do choosing, placing, and moving mics to get the right drum sound, one thing is always fundamental: the way the drummer plays, and how the drums are set up and tuned really determines the sound. Everybody is different, so we're always making minor adjustments on all the microphones to accommodate the drummer because we want him or her to be happy. When you have happy musicians, you're much more likely to get good sounds. You don't want to have a pissed-off drummer. Trust me.

Most percussionists show up at a session with a range of different things—anything you can shake or rattle can be called a percussion instrument, plus there are congas, bongos, and more traditional percussion instruments.

Percussion Table

If there is a percussion table with several things on it, I'll usually set up two AKG 414s and open them in omni so we get the little tinkly bells and the wind chimes and all that stuff—all the little toys he plays with. The table can hold anything from triangles, to cowbells, to finger cymbals, to keys, to anything you can rattle or hit.

Congas

On congas, I'll use a pair of Neumann KM 84s—I love those microphones. I place them in an "X" over the congas. Most percussionists bring two or three congas, and I'll place the two mics, and they'll form an "X" with capsules aiming down at the congas at about head-level with the percussionist. I get a very naturally balanced pick-up that way. Depending on the player, the percussionist makes most of the balance adjustments just by the way they play, whether it's Paulinho da Costa, or any of the great percussionists.

Timbales

I use two mics on timbales. I place one AKG 414 a few feet above the timbales. I also aim another 414 at the side of the timbale because it's very common for the percussionist to hit the side of the timbale as part of a rhythmic pattern.

Chimes

When there are chimes, I like to use something like an RCA 77-DX. I'll place it behind the chimes, and I'll find the position where there's a good balance of the notes being played all the way across.

Timpani

I use a Neumann U 47 fet to mike the timpani up overhead. It works really well on the timpani, I'll raise it up or lower it down depending on what kind of sound we're looking for. Sometimes I'll also use a regular U 47 in omni to get a more open sound. It can be difficult to find the right balance on the timpani because it bleeds into the rest of the microphones quite a bit.

If there is a balance problem, I'll just go to the player and say, "Listen, on that section, can you ease it a little bit for me? It's just getting a little too much." They're always happy to do whatever it takes to get the best sound. It's much easier to address the problem with the musician during the session than it is to try to fix the problem in the mix.

ACOUSTIC BASS

The acoustic bass is my favorite instrument to record—I love the acoustic bass sound. I use two Neumann M 149s: one over the f-hole from about eight inches, and one up over the finger board where the bassist plucks the strings. It doesn't really make a difference which f-hole the mic is over. It depends on the player. I always start with the f-hole on the player's left, but if you are recording a left-handed bassist, the mic might be more out of the way if it's over the f-hole on the player's right side. It sounds great either way.

Bass players always love it when I'm working on a session because I'm so conscious of getting a great bass sound. If you can't get a pair of M 149s, Neumann U 67s and U 47s also sound great on the upright bass. Right now, I think M 149s run around $4500 a piece, but they're fantastic. I know I'm repeating this, but it's important. Don't buy a bunch of cheap mics. Save your money and buy one or two really good mics. The better the microphones, the better the instrument's going to sound. That stands true for leakage from the room or other instruments, too. Because you're using such good mics, even the leakage sounds good, plus you get more of an open sound. You don't get that small, tinny sound of leakage into a cheap microphone.

One of my favorite things to record is acoustic bass using my Neumann M 149s.

I recommend using tube mics on the bass instead of solid-state because I think that approach results in a warmer tone and a better bass sound. I put the two bass mics through a pair of Summit Audio Tube Leveling Amplifier TLA-100 compressors, and I barely tap the threshold, so I get just a dB of gain reduction. I'm really using the Summit TLA-100s to get the warmth of the tube, rather than for compression.

Years ago, when we only used one mic, I'd use a Neumann U 47 or a U 67. I'd put it up between the two f-holes, just down from where the fingers pluck the strings. I did the same thing when I was using one mic. I'd run it through a tube compressor and just tap the input for about one dB of gain reduction. Like I said before, I don't like to use compression, however, I do like the sound I get running through a tube compressor. I use a compressor for the warm sound of the tube.

Neumann U 67

(FROM GEORG NEUMANN GMBH)

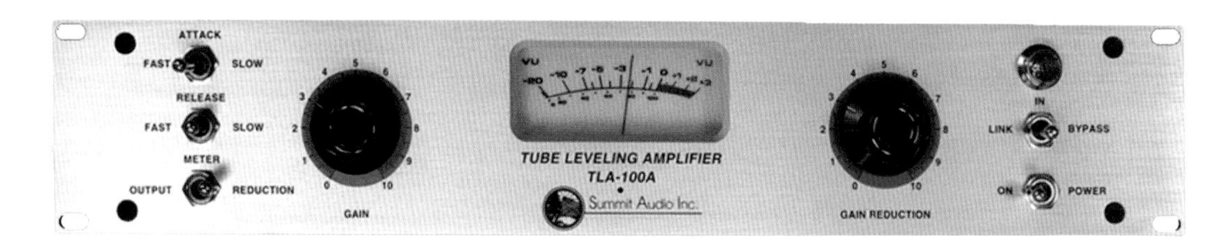

Summit Audio Tube Leveling Amplifier TLA-100

ELECTRIC BASS

On the electric bass, I have a tube direct box that I use that just sounds great. It's the Radial Firefly Tube Direct Box. Even Lee Sklar loved it when I put it on him, and he has his own stuff he brings. I'll run the bass through a compressor, and do the same thing I do with the acoustic bass—I'll set the input level and then adjust the threshold so I just tap it a little for about one dB of gain reduction.

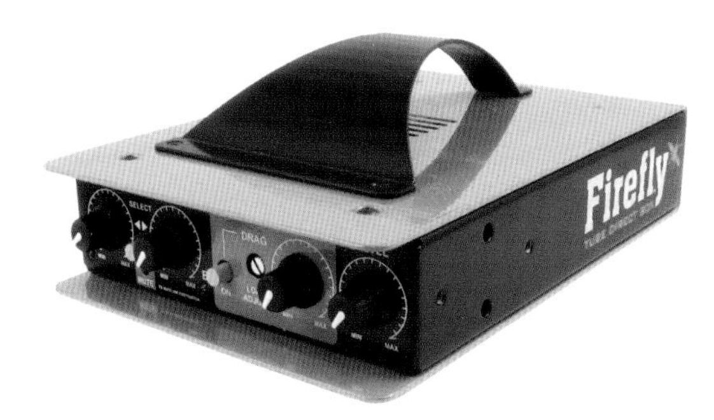

Radial Firefly Tube Direct Box

When it comes down to it, if you have a great electric bass player, you won't need to worry about much. Great players are very controlled and play very evenly so there isn't a need for much compression, if any. If the bassist wants to use an amplifier, I'll either put a condenser or ribbon microphone in front of the speaker where it sounds best to me. I love the Royer R-122 on a bass amp. And Audio-Technica makes the AT4080, a great ribbon mic that I really like a lot on a bass amp, too.

It's very important that you check phase on all microphones before you start a session. We go around to every mic with a phase clicker to make sure they're all set and in phase. And when you're miking the bass amp and running direct at the same time, it's critical that you confirm that the direct and miked tracks are in phase. Sometimes the bass amp is not in phase, so the direct and miked signals could end up fighting each other and never sound quite right.

PIANO

I did a couple albums with Joe Sample, one called *Invitation* and one called *Ashes to Ashes.* They have some of the best piano sounds I've ever gotten. If you can track those down and listen, you'll hear what a really good piano sound is. Also, I recorded an album with Bill Evans, *You Must Believe in Spring.* His trio was in the room with him, and we tried three different pianos. We had a Bösendorfer, a Steinway, and a Yamaha. We tested all three, and we wound up using the Yamaha, believe it or not. That surprised the hell out of me! But that's the piano that sounded the best in the room with that pianist.

If the featured artist is a pianist, listen to some well-respected piano albums before you go into the session. You first need to discover what the piano really should sound like. Then you'll know what you're listening for, and finding the sound just becomes a matter of choosing the right mics and putting in the right places to get that sound. If you want to adjust that sound because you're getting too much of the low end, for example, you might want to move the mic over the low strings a little farther away. It depends on the pianist and how he plays. No two players are the same, and each piece of music is different. Believe me, it's a matter of listening. Use your ears, and make sure the entire range of the piano is evenly balanced. Then, as quickly as possible, record a take, and get the pianist in the control room to hear the playback. Once the player hears what the recording sounds like, he or she will make the necessary musical adjustments, and you can agree on the right sound for the music. Recording piano is a matter of teamwork between the engineer and the pianist.

I use two M 149s on a piano pretty much all the time now. I place them about a foot above the hammers, with one mic over the high strings, and one mic over the low strings.

The first thing I think about when recording piano is the importance of the piano to the music. If I'm recording a big band, I'll use my regular setup with my M 149s. If I'm recording something with Barbra Streisand and an orchestra, I would do the same thing. This gives me what I want—a nice tight crisp sound with some attack from the hammers, and a nice low end.

UPRIGHT PIANO

On an upright piano, I always mic it from the back. I haven't recorded an upright in many years, but when I was doing a lot of Henry Mancini, he would use an upright piano for effect. I used two RCA 77-DX ribbon mics on the sounding board on the back, and that always worked well for me. You could try a lot of different things. Some guys liked to open the upright and have the mics in front, but that's never appealed to me. I've always liked picking it up from behind the piano.

HARPSICHORD

Harpsichord is dainty instrument without a lot of volume. If the harpsichordist is playing with any other instruments, you're going to want to use some isolation to minimize leakage from the other instruments. You'll need to set the input gain pretty high because the harpsichord is so quiet. That means the leakage from the other instruments will be significant without a fair amount of isolation, either with gobos, or by putting the harpsichord in another room. I always use condenser mics on the harpsichord.

ACOUSTIC GUITAR

I've been using a Neumann KM 84 on acoustic guitar for a long time. I also use the Royer R-122 on acoustic, and I love the Audio-Technica 4080 on the acoustic, too. All three of those microphones sound great on acoustic guitar.

I listen to the player out in the studio and put the mic where I think the best sound is. Then I'll go back in the control room and make sure it sounds good. I might need to go back into the studio and move the mic an inch or two to get the sound just the way I want it, and that's it. You should also trust the guitar player if they're experienced in the studio. If you're working with somebody like Dean Parks, he'll put the mic exactly where he wants to put it and it'll sound incredible. Just make sure you're using a great microphone.

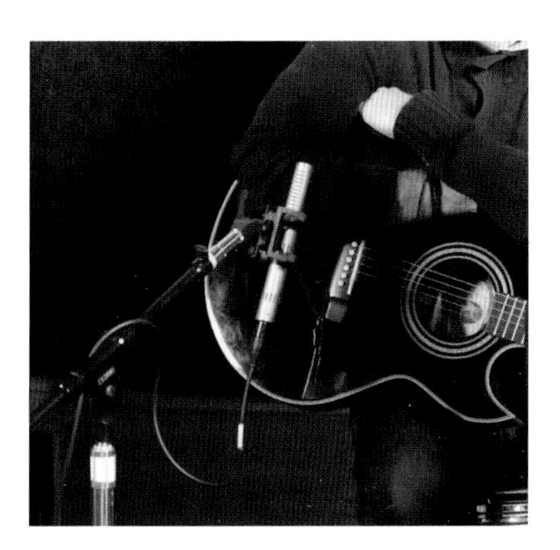

I usually use a Royer R-122 on acoustic guitar. It's important to go out in the studio and listen to find the exact spot where the guitar sounds best. That tells you where to put the mic.

I rarely use two microphones on acoustic guitar, but I have used two Neumann M 149s on a project where the artist was the acoustic player. I put the mics about two feet from the guitar, about three feet apart, and just got a great big open sound.

For big band with a Freddie Green style guitar, I just use one mic.

ELECTRIC GUITAR

If I'm recording a rhythm section, we'll usually have the amp in a booth, and I have the guitar player sitting right in front of the amp, or if he's in the studio with everyone else, we'll baffle the amp off with gobos all the way around. Most of the time, I mike the speaker with an Audio-Technica AT4080 ribbon mic. It's a great-sounding mic on electric—for that matter, it's a great-sounding mic on acoustic, too. If I don't use the 4080, I might use a Royer R-122.

If I'm recording an organ, it'll be most likely a Hammond B3 through a Leslie cabinet. I put an AKG 414 on two opposing sides of the Leslie cabinet and place them about 18–24 inches away. The 414s will be set to omni. And then on the low speaker, I use a Neumann U 47 fet. I've been doing that forever, and it seems to work, and everybody seems happy with how it sounds.

Recording Woodwinds, Brass, and Strings

SAXOPHONE

Since the beginning, I've used Neumann U 67s on sax. I love that mic on reed instruments: oboe, clarinet, baritone sax, tenor sax, and alto sax. I place the microphone in front of the instrument, aiming at the sound holes. I don't put the mic down by the bell, because the sound comes from where the holes and keys are. The sound doesn't just come from the bell, it comes from the whole instrument. So if I aim the mic at the keys from about a foot and a half away, I get the sound of the whole instrument. And I set the U 67 for an omnidirectional pickup pattern. I love the way it sounds in omni, and the 67 is always my go-to mic for woodwinds. As a matter of fact, a U 67 is my favorite mic. If somebody told me I could only use one mic to record everything with, it would be a 67. It sounds good on vocal, it sounds good on trumpet, it sounds good on saxophone, it sounds good on strings, and it sounds good on an upright bass. It is just the most versatile microphone ever made.

If I'm recording woodwinds playing with a string section, I might put just two microphones up in omni over the section. But if I'm recording a sax section in a big band date, I'll use five microphones—one U 67 in omni on each sax. Sometimes I use the Mojave MA-300. I love that microphone! I have five of them. The power supply for the Mohave has a knob that continuously varies the polar pattern from bidirectional to cardioid to omnidirectional.

Mojave MA-300

I set the mics so they're at about head-level or a little lower for the player and out front a foot or so. If they're playing saxes and flutes, I'll place the mic a little higher so it's easier for the guys to lean in closer to the mic when they play. If they're hearing a good mix, they can help with the balances.

Sometimes a soloist in a big band saxophone section might stand, so the mic will need to be just a little higher. It's teamwork. They'll work with you to find the right position. They'll try to make you as happy as possible, especially if you're keeping them happy. Working with the musicians is so important because recording is a collaborative thing—you're all working together to get the best sound for the music. Rather than fighting for a mic placement or technique, you need to get your ego out of the way, and do things in the way that foremost make everybody comfortable and happy.

I love musicians. They're usually funny and great to be around. They have great stories they love to share. And there's a lot of mutual respect. If you show them great respect, they'll show you great respect. That makes your life so much easier.

BRASS

If I'm recording trombones in a big band session, and I have four trombones, I'll use four Royer R-122s—one in front of each trombone bell, and about a foot and a half away. Trombone players like the microphone to the left of their music stand. They all like playing that way. I look at the way each player sits. Some guys are taller and shorter, but I see where their bell is, and that's where I put the mic. I'll make sure they're comfortable, and if they would like the mic a little higher or lower, I'll adjust it for them. It's most important that the players are perfectly comfortable, and then I'll put the mics where they need to go. I trust the 122s—I've been using them for years.

When I mic a trombone section, I put a Royer R-122 on each trombone, aimed at the bell.

Years ago, when I was recording all of the Mancini albums, RCA made a great cardioid ribbon mic called the 10001. It was a fabulous microphone for trombones, but they don't make them anymore. They're hard to find, and if you do find one, it's usually not in good shape. I stopped trying to use them, but the Royers are great trombone mics.

With a big band session, I like to have the trombones sitting on a riser. Then I'll put the trumpets on a higher riser behind the trombones. I use a Neumann U 67 in omni on each trumpet. Trumpet players like to have the mic just to their right of their music stand. For some reason they all like it there. I work with the trumpet players to make sure their mics are set to the right height, and even though the mics are in omni, I'm not worried about anything leaking into the trumpet mics, because the trumpets are so loud.

Royer R-122 ribbon microphone

RCA 10001 (KU-3A) cardioid ribbon microphone (PHOTO BY STANLEY COUTANT)

I'll also put a microphone above and in front of the trumpet, and about ten feet away. That mic could be anything from a stereo Royer ribbon mic to an AKG C12 VR, which I would set to omni. That way I'm capturing the room sound that I can blend in with the close mics if that's what I need in the mix. I'll also put two microphones up over the conductor, and about ten feet up. I use them like a Decca Tree, only with two mics instead of three. I'll put those in omni, and I'll use 149s or M 50s if I can get them. I use those mics to get the distant room-sound.

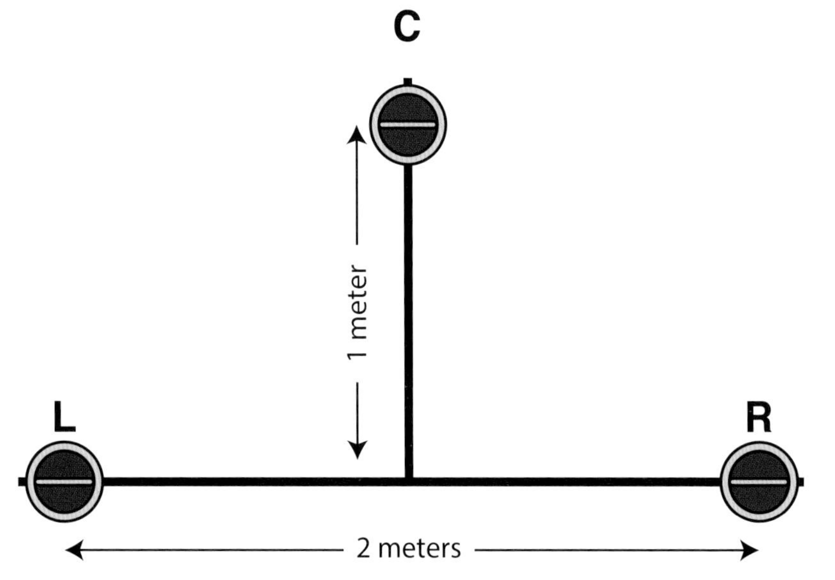

I put two omni mics on a Decca Tree, above the conductor. I use the left and right position on the Decca Tree but not the center position.

With the close mics and the distant mics in place, the rest is a matter of mixing—finding the best musical balance. I can create the balances that I want, changing the coloring as I'm mixing. If the arrangement is really tight and clean, I'll use less of the room. If there's a big open tutti section, I'll add more of the room to capture more of that open big sound.

STRINGS

If I'm recording a large string section, the first thing I do is put a couple Neumann M 50s about five to ten feet above the conductor's head, or I might use a Decca Tree with M 50s. On the violins, depending on how big the section is, I'll use from two to four omnidirectional Neumann U 67s about ten feet up over the section. Depending on how many violas there are, there will be one or two omni U 67s over the violas, positioned the same way as the mics over the violins—eight to ten feet above the section. I'll handle the celli a little differently. On the celli, lately, I've been using the Audio-Technica 4080 ribbon microphone, with one mic on each two celli. So if there are six celli, there will be three microphones, all placed up over the stand, and facing down toward each two celli. If there are arco basses, they'll be behind the celli and I'll use U 47s—one U 47 for two basses, and two U 47s if there are four basses. I set all the mics to omni—obviously except the ribbons on the celli, which are bidirectional simply by design.

I always work with the arranger and conductor to find the right balance. Again, it's always best if you work as a team. If I want less celli in one part of the arrangement, rather than just turning the celli mics down at bar 45 (for example), I'll talk to the conductor, and then at bar 45 he'll have the cellists play softer. If the conductor makes that change, it will sound much more natural than if I need to raise and lower microphones levels. So I set my microphones up and get a great overall sound on everything. Then it's a matter of the conductor and I working together. If the French horns are too loud in one section, he'll keep them down in that section. If I need more in a certain section, the conductor will have them play a little louder. That way I'm not constantly trying to follow the score and riding gain on everything. It sounds so much better when the balances are controlled in the room. If I turn the faders up or down, I'm affecting the instrument balance, but I'm also affecting the balance of the room with the instruments. Also, when a musician pays louder or more quietly, the tone of the instrument and his or her musical expression and interpretation changes.

Al's Tool Chest

MICROPHONES

Neumann U 47 and U 48

The original Neumann U 47 was also released under the Telefunken name in 1947. Most people don't know that the iconic U 47 at Capitol Studios in Los Angeles that was used by Frank Sinatra, Paul McCartney, Diana Krall and many others, is actually a U 48. (FROM GEORG NEUMANN GMBH)

Released in May of 1948, the Neumann U 48 is identical in every way to the U 47, with the exception of their directional characteristics (U 47: non-directional and cardioid; U 48: bidirectional and cardioid), which can easily be selected by means of a slide-switch located at the base of the wire-mesh part of the microphones. The newer type U 48 is designed in such a way that the plug-in head of the U 47 may be inserted in place of the U 48 head, thus making possible all three patterns within the same basic unit, whereas it is impossible to use the U 48 head in place of the U 47 head. (FROM GEORG NEUMANN GMBH)

Operating Principle. Large-diaphragm condenser (tube)

Al's Preferred Applications. Vocal, upright bass, timpani (omni).

A Note from Al. There's just a quality to the U 47 that no other mic has. I don't care how many people try to duplicate it, there's just something special about that microphone. It's hard to put your finger on it, but everybody that sings on that mic just loves it, because it brings out a great quality in the voice. Even though it's not easy to describe the sound in words, I just know that when I put the U 47 up and somebody starts singing, it's special. I'll do shoot-outs, especially with female voices, but 90 percent of the time, the 47 sounds best. It does a good job of capturing a very smooth high-end, but there's also something in the resonance that brings out a fantastic quality in the voice. It enhances the vocal, whether you're singing or talking into the microphone. If you look at the frequency response graph, that might say something. I know it's not a super flat microphone.

Frequency Response and Polar Pattern

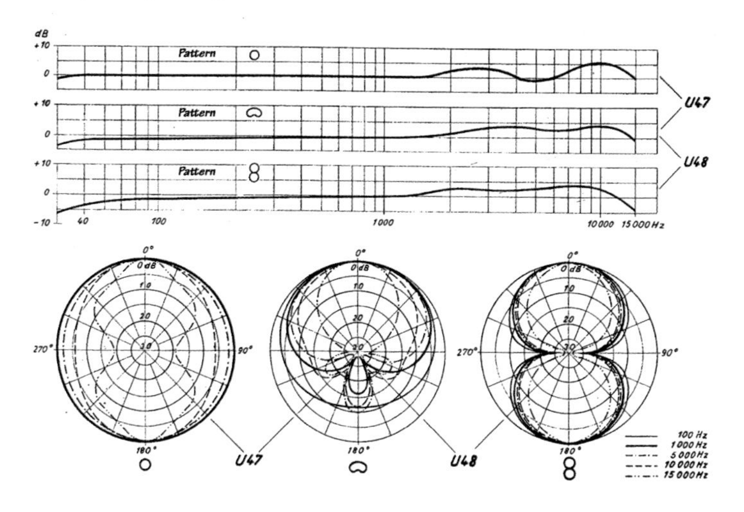

The frequency response graphs and polar patterns for the Neumann U 47 and U 48 (FROM GEORG NEUMANN GMBH)

Technical Data

MICROPHONES:

Useable range of frequencies	35–15,000 cps
Directional Characteristics U 47	Non-directional and cardioid
Directional Characteristics U 48	Bidirectional and cardioid
Source impedance	200 or 50 ohms
Sensitivity U 47	Approx. 2.5 mv/dyne/cm2 (cardioid)
Sensitivity U 48	Approx. 2.0 mv/dyne/cm2 (cardioid)
Total Harmonic Distortion	Less than 0.8% (at 1000 cps) up to a sound pressure level of 110 dB
Tube Complement	1 VF-14 M (selected)
Power Requirement	110/120 volts 50–60 cps
Operating Voltage	105 volts D.C. (40 ma) (the heater voltage is taken from the 105 volt supply)

(SOURCE: GEORG NEUMANN GMBH)

Neumann U 47 fet

Neumann U 47 fet
(FROM GEORG NEUMANN GMBH)

Operating Principle. Large-diaphragm condenser (field-effect transistor)

Al's Preferred Applications. Bass drum, timpani, low speaker of a Leslie cabinet.

A Note from Al. When the U 47 fet came out, I didn't like it. I used it for something like a kick drum or the low end of an organ. I didn't have any use for it on horns or vocals or anything like that. The 47 fet is just not one of my favorite mics. However, if I set up to record a Leslie speaker, I'll mic the low speaker with the U 47 fet. It's my go-to mic for that purpose—it gives me exactly what I want. I'll also use the 47 fet as overheads for timpani. What I like about the mic is its ability to handle a lot of low end. To my ear, it seems to enhance the low end.

Frequency Response and Polar Pattern

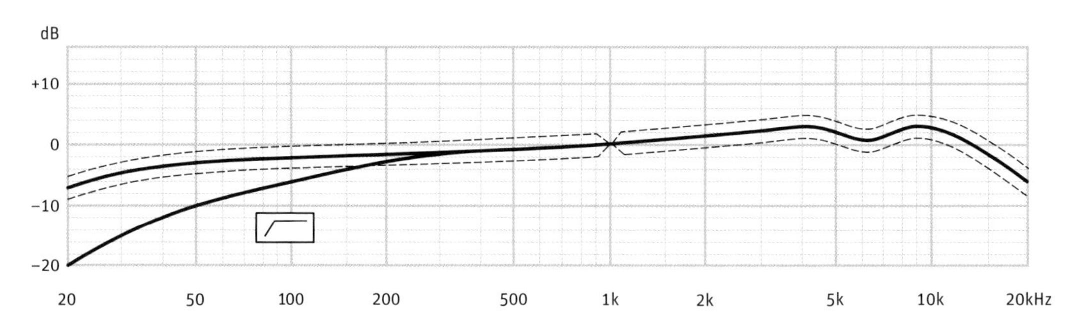

U 47 fet frequency response (FROM GEORG NEUMANN GMBH)

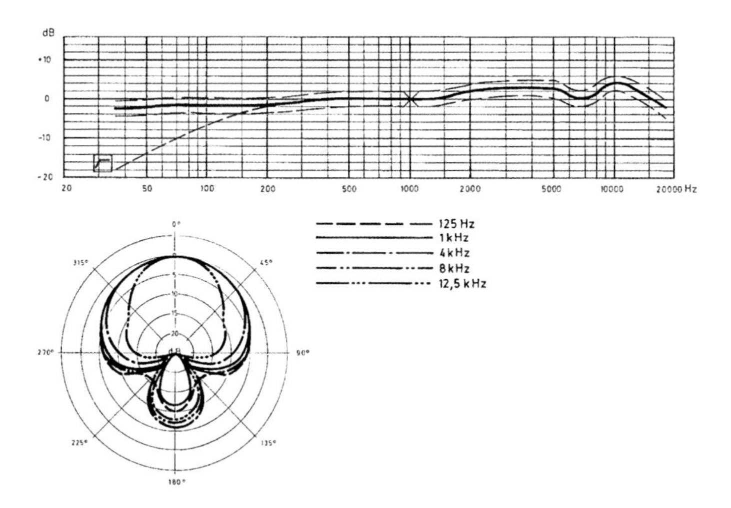

U 47 fet polar pattern (FROM GEORG NEUMANN GMBH)

Technical Data

Acoustic operating principle	pressure gradient transducer
Polar pattern	supercardioid
Frequency range	42–16,000 Hz
Sensitivity	8 mV/PA ± dB
Source impedance	150 ohms
Minimum load impedance	750 ohms
S/N ratio according to DIN 45 590 (ref. Level 1 Pa)	69 dB
Equivalent noise weighted noise level according to DIN 45 590	25 dB
A-weighted equivalent loudness level due to inherit noise (IEC 179, DIN 45 634)	
Max SPL for 0.5% THD at 1 kHz with sensitivity reduction max. output voltage	137 dB ≙ 141 Pa 147 dB ≙ 147 Pa 1128 mV
Power supply (P 48 DIN 45 596)	48V ± 4V phantom powering
Current consumption	0.5 mA
Minimum operating time on batteries	15 hours
Weight	710 g (25 ounces)

Neumann U 67

Al's favorite mic, the Neumann U 67

The power supply for the Neumann U 67 (PHOTO BY STANLEY COUTANT)

Operating Principle. Large-diaphragm condenser (tube)

Al's Preferred Applications. Bass (one mic), vocal, guitar, woodwinds, trumpet, string section, violins, violas.

A Note from Al. If I could only have one microphone, I'd choose the U 67. It sounds great on everything. It's a completely versatile mic. First of all, it takes a beating. I can set it two or three feet in front of a trumpet player when he's just blowing his brains out, and the U 67 holds up great. It has a 10 dB pad built in, and you can set it to omni, cardioid, or figure-8. I use it on strings all the time because there's a quality to the mic that gives violins and violas a richness that I like.

I use it on solo saxophones all the time, and sometimes I'll use it on solo trumpet. I always use four U 67s on the trumpets in a big band, and I use five of them on the saxophones. They sound great in omni. I always set the four trumpet mics and five sax mics to omni when I'm recording big band. The blend is great when you can hear the bleed of the first tenor into the lead alto mic or the second trumpet into the first trumpet mic. It just has a great blend. You could use the 67 on a guitar amp, and if it were loud, you could put the 10 dB pad on, but mostly I steer away from using tube mics on amplifiers. Nowdays, I'm more likely to use a ribbon mic on a guitar amplifier.

Frequency Response and Polar Pattern

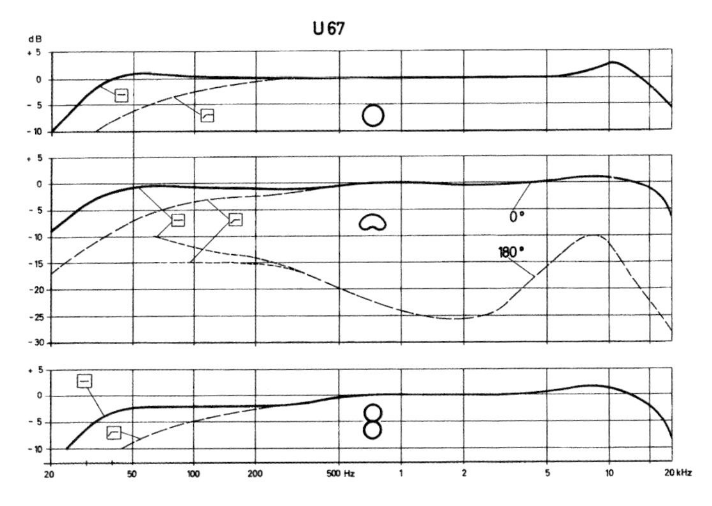

Neumann U 67 frequency response (FROM GEORG NEUMANN GMBH)

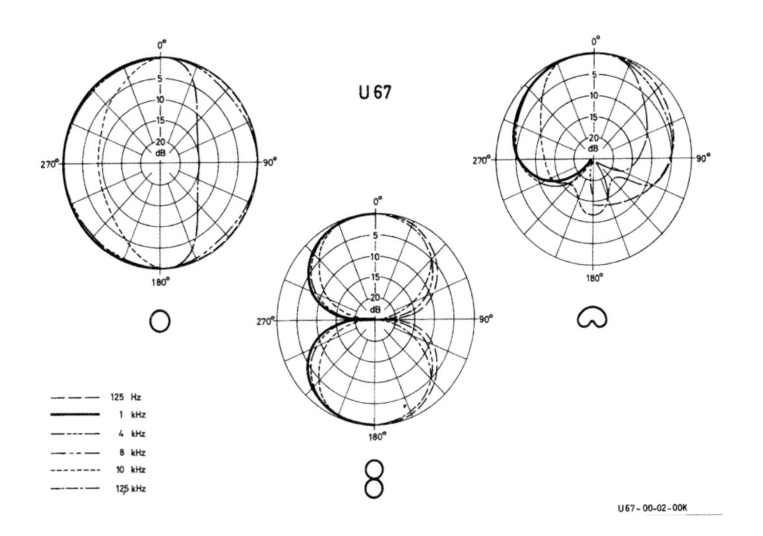

Neumann U 67 polar response (FROM GEORG NEUMANN GMBH)

Technical Data

Acoustical system	Combination of two pressure transducers, electrically switchable to omnidirectional, cardioid, and figure-8
Frequency range	30–16,000 cps
Output levels	Omnidirectional: 1.1 mV/µb across 1000 Ω Cardioid: 2.0 mV/µb across 1000 Ω Figure-8: 1.4 mV/µb across 1000 Ω
Electrical load resistance	≥1000 Ω (250) Ω
Electrical source resistance	approx. 1 x 50pF (cardioid) approx. 2 x 50pF (omnidirectional, figure-8)
Capacitance of capsule	approx. 1 x 50pF (cardioid) approx. 2 x 50pF (omnidirectional, figure-8)
Stray voltage	≤7 µV
Noise voltage	≤5,5 µV (measured with DIN 45 405) ≙25 dB (cardioid) ≙28 dB (omnidirectional, figure-8) above 2 x 10-4 µb
Maximum sound pressure for 0.5 % harmonic distortion at 40, 1000, and 5000 cps	≥125 µb ≙116 dB (if initially attenuated, approx. 400 µb)
Amplification of preamplifier	-2.0 dB (cardioid) 0 dB (omnidirectional, figure-8)
Switchable attenuation	approx. 10 dB
Impedance of calibrating input	600 unbalanced
Tubes	1 x EF 86
Dimensions	201 mm length 56 mm diameter
Weight	0.54 kg

(SOURCE: GEORG NEUMANN GMBH)

Neumann M 49 and M 50

The Neumann M 49 (right) and M 50 (left). The multi-pattern M 49 has a red dot and the omni-only M 50 has a white dot.
(FROM GEORG NEUMANN GMBH)

Operating Principle. Large-diaphragm condenser (tube)

Al's Preferred Applications. Vocal (M 49), orchestra (M 50).

A Note from Al. I love the M 49. That's the microphone we used on Barbra Streisand on *The Way We Were* album—it's Barbra's favorite mic. If Barbra hadn't had an opinion about the M 49, I probably would have used the 47, but to be honest, there isn't really that much different between those two mics. The 47 is a little smaller than the 49, so it doesn't take up as much space in front of the singer, but with Barbra that didn't matter.

On so many of the Mancini albums that I recorded in the '60s, I would put two M 49s up, set the pattern to figure-8, and record the sax section with two saxes on one side and three saxes on the other—that's the way we got our blend. We'd record a little bit and then listen back with the band. Then we might have one guy step in a little, and another step back, until the blend was perfect. Hank (Mancini) used a lot of bass flute parts, and with this mic setup and the M 49s, when it was time for the bass flutes solo, the player would just lean in and we'd get this great bass flute sound!

The M 50 is an amazing microphone. I use them on a Decca Tree to record strings and orchestral music. They are definitely the go-to mics for recording strings with a Decca Tree. The standard Decca Tree has left, center, and middle positions with each mic one meter away from the other. I just use the left and right positions so the mics are two meters apart. A lot of the sound comes from how we set the room up. Almost every serious film scoring engineer uses a Decca Tree with M 50s.

There really isn't anything else I'd use them for, but they are the best for recording an orchestra. When I use them, I have a friend who loans them to me, because I don't own any and neither does Capitol. They're really very expensive.

The M 50 has a warmth to it that's unique, and it has a smoother sound. It's not like you can set the M 49 to omni and expect to get the same results as using an M 50, which is exclusively omni. They're just different-sounding mics. The 49 has a top-end brightness to it that the 50 doesn't have. But even though the mics sound different, if I didn't have the M 50s I would use the M 49s instead. (From Georg Neumann GmbH)

Polar Pattern and Frequency Response

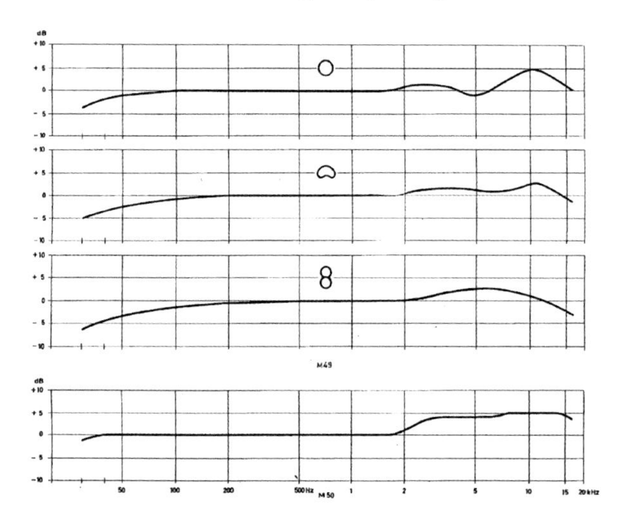

Neumann M 49 frequency response (FROM GEORG NEUMANN GMBH)

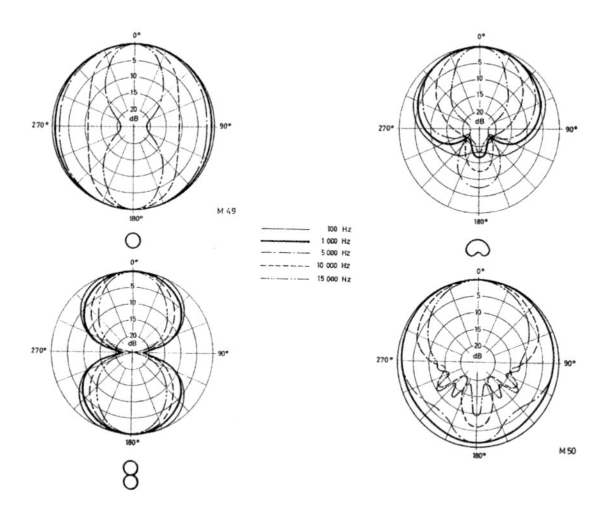

Neumann M 49 polar pattern (FROM GEORG NEUMANN GMBH)

Technical Data M 49

Useable frequency range	40–15,000 cps
Directional characteristic	Non-directional, cardioid, bidirectional
Sensitivity	approx. 0.7 mv/dyne/cm2 at 1000 ohms
Total harmonic distortion	Less than 0.6% (40–15,000 cps) up to a sound pressure level of 114 dB
Source impedance	200 or 50 ohms
Tube complement	1 Telefunken AC 701k (selected)

(SOURCE: GEORG NEUMANN GMBH)

Technical Data M 50

Useable frequency range	40–15,000 cps
Directional characteristic	Non-directional
Sensitivity	approx. 0.7 mv/dyne/cm2 at 1000 ohms
Total harmonic distortion	Less than 0.6% (40–15,000 cps) up to a sound pressure level of 114 dB
Source impedance	200 or 50 ohms
Tube complement	1 Telefunken AC 701k (selected)

(SOURCE: GEORG NEUMANN GMBH)

Neumann M 149

Neumann M 149
(FROM GEORG NEUMANN GMBH

Operating Principle. Large-diaphragm condenser (tube)

Al's Preferred Applications. Choir, upright bass, piano, stereo acoustic guitar.

A Note from Al. There's a top end to the M 149 that I love. There's a brightness to the sound. It's very crisp, but it's not strident. There's a smoothness to it that I really like a lot. It's been a go-to mic ever since they first came out. I have five of them now. I've been using them on upright bass, and every bass player in town that works with me always comes in and gives me a hug and a kiss on the cheek because they love the sound so much. It's the same thing on the piano. They just sound amazing on piano, too. I would also use the AKG C12 VR on piano, but I really like the M 149s better.

I don't use them too much for acoustic guitar, though I did do a very nice stereo recording on an acoustic guitar, and I used a pair of 149s for that. For miking acoustic guitar, I have three mics that I go to all the time: the Royer R-122, the AT4080, and the AT5045, which is a great mic.

Frequency Response and Polar Pattern

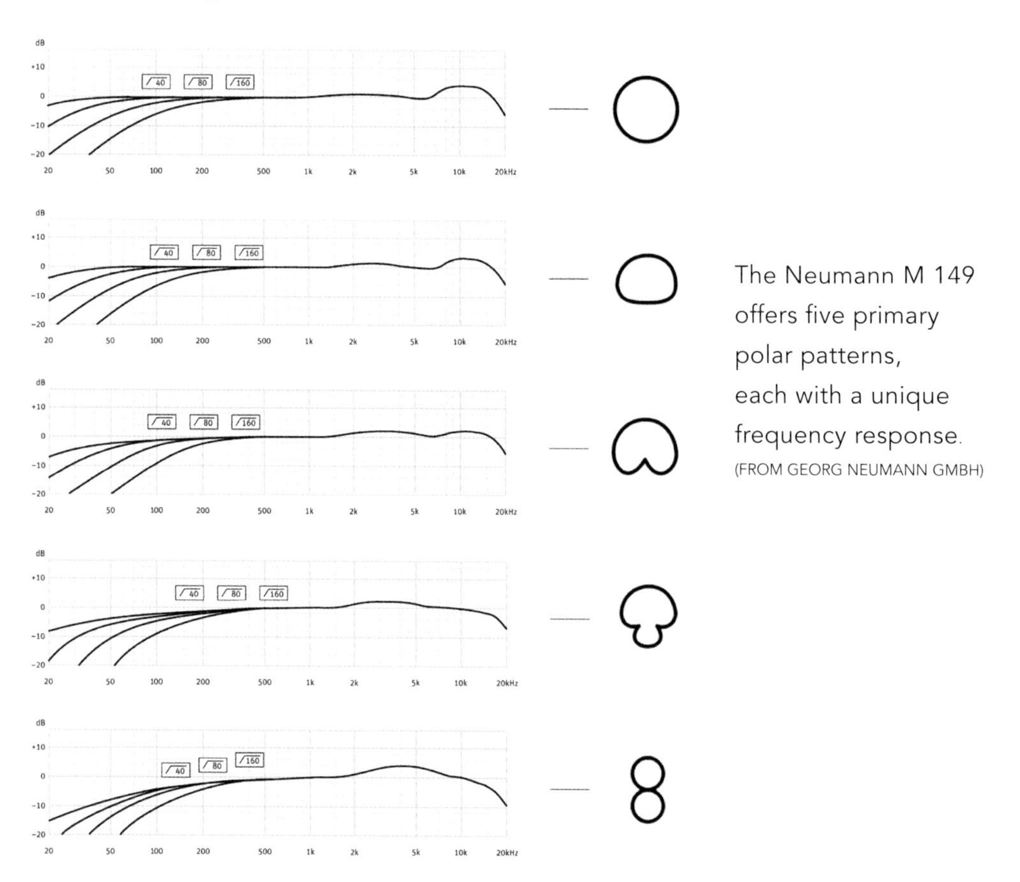

The Neumann M 149 offers five primary polar patterns, each with a unique frequency response. (FROM GEORG NEUMANN GMBH)

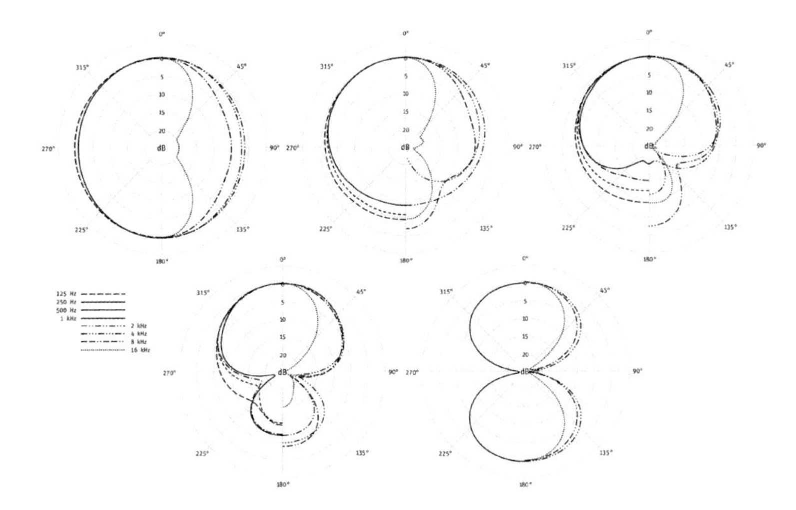

The Neumann M 149 has five primary polar patterns (omni, wide angle cardioid, cardioid, hypercardioid, figure-8) and four additional intermediate patterns. (FROM GEORG NEUMANN GMBH)

Technical Data

Acoustical operating principle	Pressure gradient
Polar pattern	Omni, wide-angle cardioid, cardioid, hypercardioid, figure-8 and 4 additional intermediate patterns
Frequency response	20 Hz–20 kHz
Sensitivity	34/4 7 /62 mV /Pa2)
Nominal impedance	50 ohms
Nominal load impedance	1000 ohms
Signal-to-noise ratio, CCIR	66/69/71 dB
Signal-to-noise ratio, A-weighted	78/81/83 dB
Equivalent noise level, CCIR	28/25/23 dB
Equivalent noise level, A-weighted	16/13/11 dB-A
Max. SPL (tube characteristic)	
for THD< 0.5%	120 dB
for THD< 5%	136 dB
Dynamic range of the amplifier (cardioid) A-weighted	
for THD<0.5%	101 dB
for THD< 5%	121 dB
Max. output voltage	18 dBu

(SOURCE: GEORG NEUMANN GMBH)

Neumann KM 84

Neumann KM 84 small-diaphragm condenser mic
(FROM GEORG NEUMANN GMBH)

Operating Principle. Small-diaphragm condenser

Al's Preferred Applications. Congas, percussion.

A Note from Al. I love the KM 84. I use it on percussion a lot, on congas and timbales, and I use it on the toys (percussionists bring a table filled with a myriad of toys—things like triangle and finger cymbals, and pretty much anything that they can hit, slap, or rattle for a unique sound). I like the fact that it's a small microphone, and that's easy to position without taking up a lot of space and getting in the musician's way. I've used it on acoustic guitar, but not too often. The KM 84 is a great microphone, and it'll work on pretty much anything, but I've really liked using it for percussion.

Frequency Response and Polar Pattern

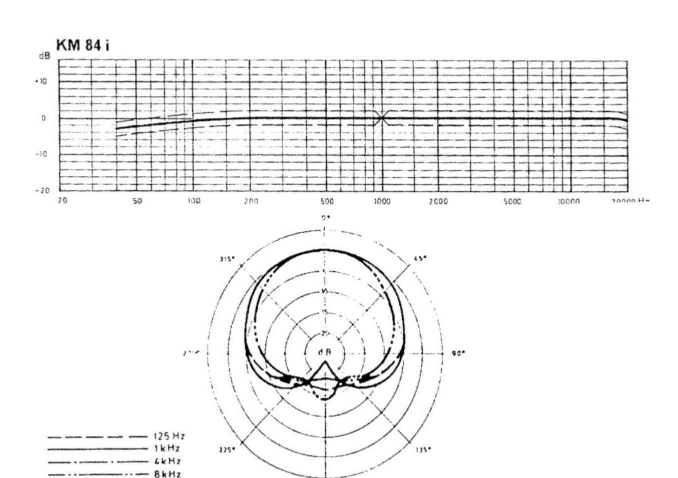

Neumann KM 84 Frequency Response and Polar Response
(FROM GEORG NEUMANN GMBH)

Technical Data

Acoustical operating principle	Pressure gradient transducer
Polar pattern	Cardioid
Frequency response	40 Hz–18 kHz
Sensitivity at 1 kHz	5
Nominal impedance	150 ohms
Nominal load impedance	1000 ohms
Signal-to-noise ratio, CCIR	69 dB
Max. SPL for less than 0.5% THD at 1 kHz with pre-attenuation dB	123 dB
Power supply	48V ±4V
Current consumption	0.4 mA
Weight	80 g

(SOURCE: GEORG NEUMANN GMBH)

Telefunken ELA M 251

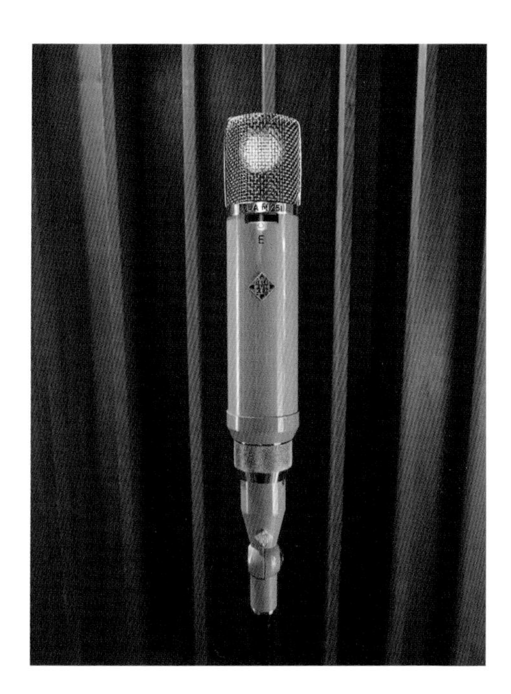

Telefunken
ELA M 251

Operating Principle. Large-diaphragm condenser (tube)

Al's Preferred Applications. Vocals

A Note from Al. The Telefunken 251 is a fabulous microphone. I don't own any of them and Capitol doesn't have any, but Bill Schnee has several of them at his studio (Schnee Studio in North Hollywood), and when I've worked there, I used them a lot. They are incredible microphones. They work very well on vocals for certain artists, and they have a character that's similar to the U 47.

Technical Data

Type	Pressure Gradient Condenser
Capsule	CK12 - 25mm Edge Terminated Diaphragm
Tube Type	GE JAN 6072a (NOS)
Transformer	Haufe T14/1
Polar Pattern	cardioid, omnidirectional, and bidirectional
Frequency Range	20 Hz –20 kHz, ± 3 dB
Sensitivity	17mV/pa ± 1 dB
THD at 1kHZ at 1Pa (Amplifier)	< 0.2%
Output Impedance	200 Ω
Maximum SPL (for 1% THD)	130 dB
S/N Ratio	85 dBA
Self Noise (Amplifier)	9dBA
Dimensions	216 mm L x 50 mm diameter
Weight	596 g
Current Draw from Mains	80 mA
Cable	M 850E 25-ft Sommer Cable, Vintage Compatible 6 Pin Female Stand Mount, 7 Pin Male XLR

(SOURCE: TELEFUNKEN ELEKTROAKUSTIK)

Frequency Response and Polar Pattern

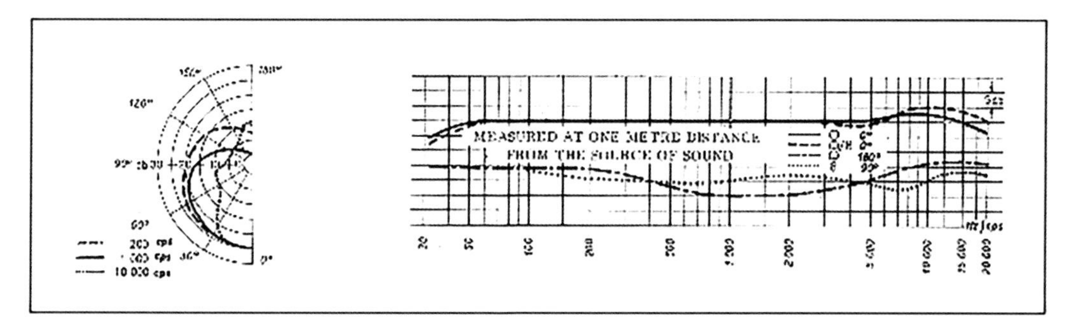

Telefunken 251 Frequency Response and Polar Pattern

Brauner VM1

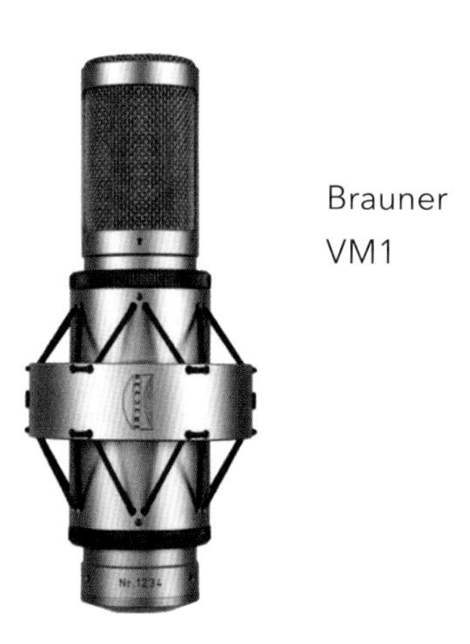

Brauner VM1

Operating Principle. Large-diaphragm condenser (tube)

Al's Preferred Applications. Vocal, sax solo, any solo, cello, violin.

A Note from Al. I love the Brauner VM1. I have a fondness for that, because years ago I was doing a big session in Berlin with Alan Bergman. Dirk knew I was there and he brought me a bunch of Brauner microphones to use on the session. I love my VM1. It's a terrific all-around microphone. It's not just for vocals, although I seem to recall using it on Natalie Cole. When I first got the mic, I used it on vocals quite a bit, but I would also use it on a saxophone solo, or any solo instrument, like a cello or violin.

Polar Pattern Graphs and Frequency Response Charts. Dirk Brauner doesn't believe that charts have value, so they don't publish them. The VM1 polar pattern is infinitely variable on the external power supply, from omnidirectional, to bidirectional, to cardioid.

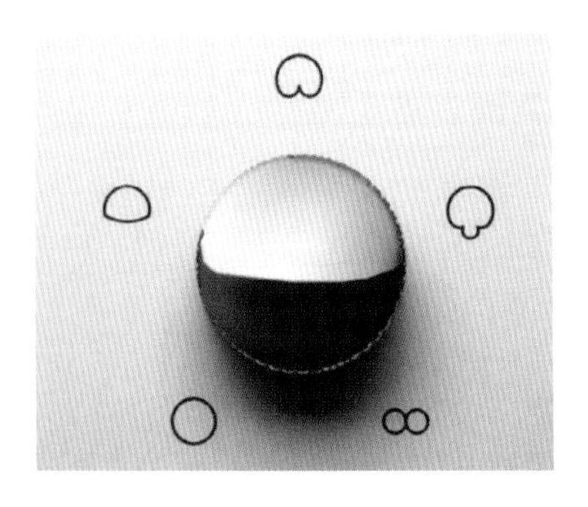

The Brauner VM1 polar pattern selector

Technical Data

Microphone Category::	Tube Microphone
Pattern	Any/Continuously Variable
Acoustical Principle:	Large diaphragm condenser microphone
Frequency Range	20 Hz–22 kHz
Sensitivity:	28 mV/Pa @ 1 kHz @ 1m
Impedance:	200 Ohm
Self Noise:	< 11 dB A (IEC 651)
Signal to Noise:	> 83 dB A (1 Pa/1kHz cardioid)
Maximum SPL:	142 dB SPL @ 0.3% THD
Included in delivery:	Microphone, Suspension, PSU/remote w/ Cable, VOVOX TubeLink Cable 7.5m, Windscreen (not for "pure cardioid" versions), Manual, Aluminum Case

(SOURCE: BRAUNER MICROPHONES)

Audio-Technica AT5040

Audio-Technica
5040

Operating Principle. Large four-part diaphragm condenser

Al's Preferred Applications. Vocals

A Note from Al. A lot of engineers use the 5040 on vocals. Its strength is on female vocals. When we record a new vocalist, I always set up a few different mics to try, and the 5040 is often one of those mics.

Technical Data

Element	Fixed-charge back plate, permanently polarized condenser
Polar Patten	Cardioid
Frequency Response	20–20,000 Hz
Open Circuit Sensitivity	–25 dB (56.2 mV) re: 1V at 1Pa
Impedance	50 ohms
Maximum Input Sound Level	142 dB SPL, 1 kHz at 1% T.H.D.
Noise	5 dB SPL
Dynamic Range (typical)	137 dB, 1 kHz at Max SPL
Signal-to-Noise Ratio	89 dB, 1 kHz at 1 Pa
Phantom Power Requirements	48V DC, 3.8 mA typical
Weight	582 g (20.5 oz)

Dimensions	165.3 mm (6.51") long, 57.0 mm (2.24") maximum body diameter
Output Connectors	Integral 3-pin XLRM-type
Accessories Furnished	AT8480 shock mount for 5/8"-27 threaded stands; protective carrying case

(SOURCE: AUDIO-TECHNICA)

Frequency Response and Polar Pattern

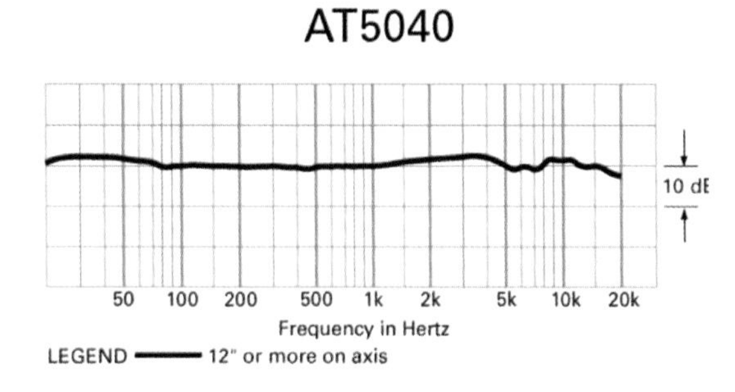

AT 5040 Frequency response

Audio-Technica 5045

Audio-Technica AT5045

Operating Principle. Large-diaphragm condenser

Al's Preferred Applications. Drum overheads, acoustic guitar

A Note from Al. I use the 5045 on drum overheads and they sound fantastic. There's a crispness to the sound, and the cymbals sound great. I'll use it on acoustic guitar sometimes. The thing I like about this mic is that it sounds so clear and bright but still smooth. It's really nice.

Frequency Response and Polar Pattern

frequency response: 20–20,000 Hz

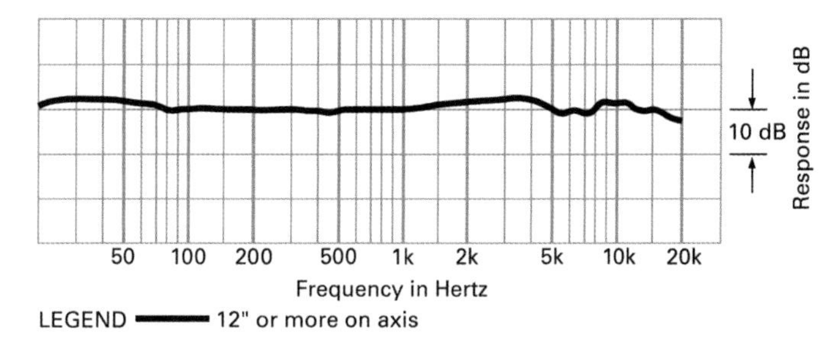

AT5045 Frequency response

polar pattern

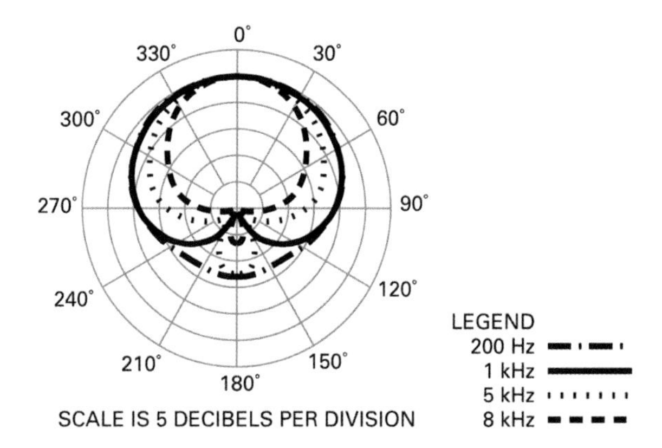

AT5045 Polar response

Technical Data

Element	Fixed-charge back plate, permanently polarized condenser
Polar pattern	Cardioid
Frequency response	20–20,000 Hz
Open circuit sensitivity	–35 dB (17.7 mV) re 1V at 1 Pa
Impedance	100 ohms
Maximum input sound level	149 dB SPL, 1 kHz at 1% T.H.D.
Noise	8 dB SPL
Dynamic range (typical)	141 dB, 1 kHz at Max SPL
Signal-to-noise ratio	86 dB, 1 kHz at 1 Pa
Phantom power requirements	48V DC, 1.4 mA typical
Weight	197 g (7.0 oz.)
Dimensions	177.0 mm (6.97") long, 25.0 mm (0.98") maximum body diameter

(SOURCE: AUDIO-TECHNICA)

Audio-Technica 5047

Audio-Technica
AT5047

Operating Principle. Large four-part diaphragm condenser

Al's Preferred Applications. Vocals

A Note from Al. The AT5047 is an excellent vocal mic. I found it when Steve Genewick and I were in France teaching a seminar. Audio-Technica had sent it to the studio so we could test it out. We plugged the mic in to try it on a male vocalist, and as soon I opened the mic, I looked at Steve, and he looked me, and we were both amazed at how great it sounded, and everyone in the room agreed. We didn't even try another mic because the 5047 just sounded fantastic.

Frequency Response and Polar Pattern

frequency response: 20–20,000 Hz

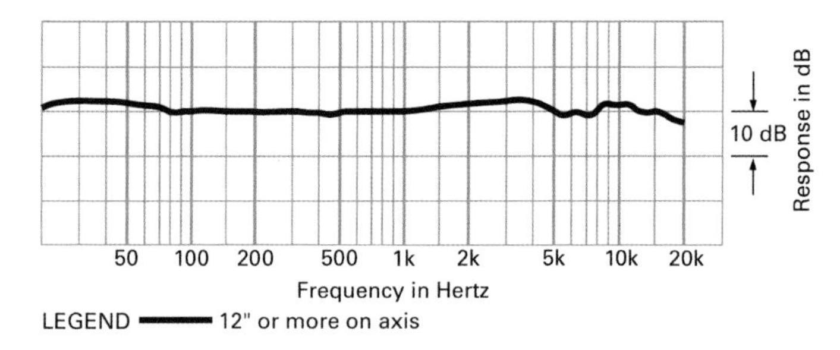

AT5047 frequency response

polar pattern

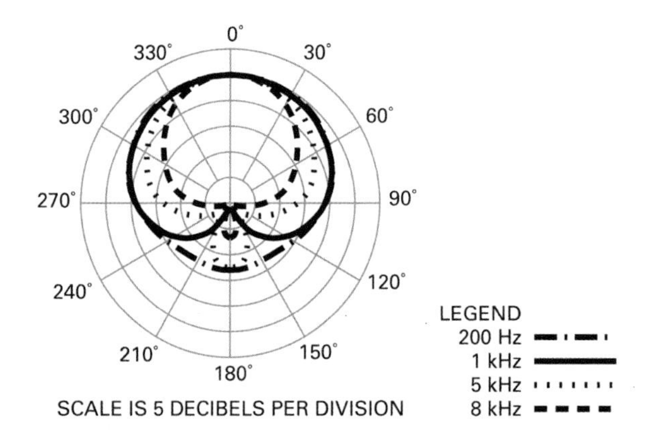

AT5047 polar pattern

Technical Data

Element	Fixed-charge back plate, permanently polarized condenser
Polar pattern	Cardioid
Frequency response	20–20,000 Hz
Open circuit sensitivity	-29 dB (35.5 mV) re 1V at 1 Pa
Impedance	150 ohms
Maximum input sound level	148 dB SPL, 1 kHz at 1% T.H.D.
Noise1	6 dB SPL
Dynamic range (typical)	142 dB, 1 kHz at Max SPL
Signal-to-noise ratio1	88 dB, 1 kHz at 1 Pa
Phantom power requirements	48V DC, 2.7 mA typical
Weight	592 g (20.9 oz)
Dimensions	165.3 mm (6.51") long, 57.0 mm (2.24") maximum body diameter
Output connector	Integral 3-pin XLRM-type
Audio-Technica case style	R10
Accessories furnished	AT8480 shock mount for 5/8"-27 threaded stands; 3/8" to 5/8" stand adapter; protective carrying case

(SOURCE: AUDIO-TECHNICA)

Audio-Technica AT4080

Audio-Technica AT4080 ribbon microphone

Operating Principle. Ribbon

Al's Preferred Applications. Bass amp, guitar amp, acoustic guitar, celli section

A Note from Al. The 4080 is a great-sounding ribbon mic, and it takes a punch. It'll handle very loud sources without a problem, and there's a nice smooth quality to the microphone. I like the 4080 a lot. If you listen to the Dylan recordings on *Triplicate*, the electric guitar and steel guitar are all recorded with the AT4080. The mic was six to eight inches from each speaker cabinet, and I didn't use any EQ. In fact, I virtually never use EQ on material that I recorded. The only time I'll use EQ is when I'm mixing something that I didn't record and I need to get a sound that I want.

I like the 4080 a lot for acoustic guitar, too. And I use it all the time on celli with one 4080 for every two celli. So if we have six celli, we put three mics on them, and put the mics four to five feet away.

Frequency Response and Polar Pattern

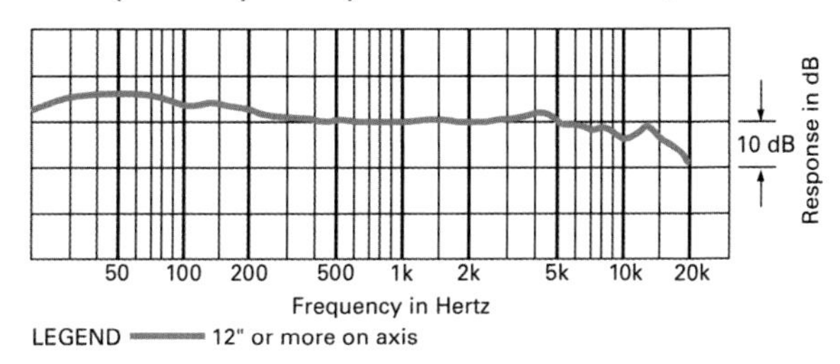

AT4080 frequency response

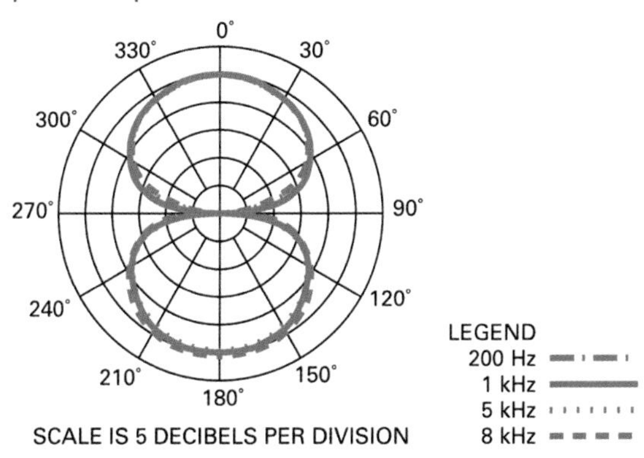

AT4080 polar pattern

Technical Data

Element	Ribbon
Polar pattern	Figure-of-eight
Frequency response	20–18,000 Hz
Open circuit sensitivity	–39 dB (11.2 mV) re 1V at 1 Pa
Impedance	100 ohms
Maximum input sound level	150 dB SPL, 1 kHz at 1% T.H.D.
Noise	22 dB SPL
Dynamic range (typical)	128 dB, 1 kHz at Max SPL
Signal-to-noise ratio	72 dB, 1 kHz at 1 Pa
Phantom power requirements	48V DC, 3.0 mA typical
Weight	474 g (16.7 oz)
Dimensions	177.5 mm (6.99") long, 53.4 mm (2.10")

(SOURCE: AUDIO-TECHNICA)

Electro-Voice Model 666

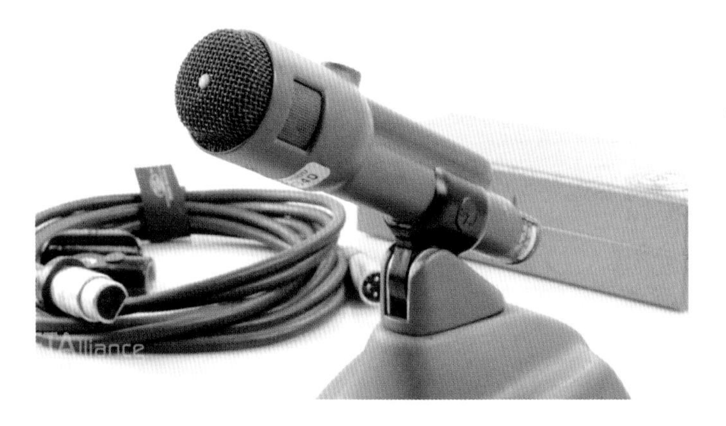

Electro-Voice 666 dynamic microphone

Operating Principle. Dynamic

Al's Preferred Applications. None

A Note from Al. Really, I was surprised we were even doing a vocal tune on George Benson's *Breezin'* album because George, to that point, was an instrumental act. When they said they wanted to do a vocal, we didn't have an appropriate vocal mic set up, so I just looked around and saw the 666 sitting on a stand, and I just grabbed it and put it in front of George. I have no idea why it was there. I assumed that when the session was set up, somebody put a few extra microphones around the room just in case we needed them.

The band was all in the same room, and George was right next to the drums. I figured we would overdub the vocal later, but he just killed it. That was the only take, and he nailed it, and it wasn't going to get any better! That was it. On the next album I recorded with George, I had a hard time getting him to try another microphone.

I ended up getting that microphone from Capitol and donating it to the Grammy Museum.

Polar Pattern and Frequency Response

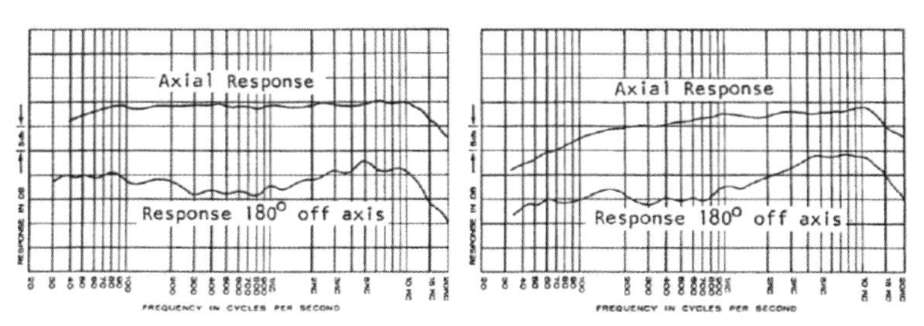

Electro-Voice Model 666 frequency response

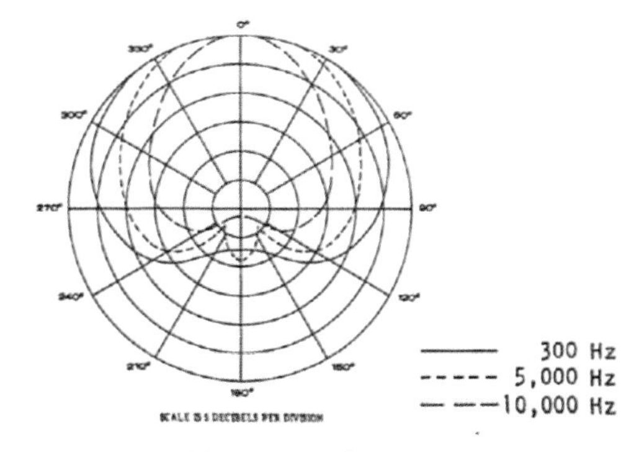

Electro-Voice Model 666 polar pattern

Technical Data

Generating Element:	Dynamic
Frequency Response:	Model 666: 40–15, 000 Hz Model 666R: 40–15, 000 Hz (rising 4-1/2 dB 100–1,000 Hz)
Output Level:	Model 666 Impedance rating 50 ohm: -58 dB* EIA sensitivity: -151 dB 150 ohm: - 58 dB* EIA sensitivity: -152 dB 250 ohm: -58 dB* EIA sensitivity: -150 dB Model 666R ImpedanceRating 50 ohm: - 56 dB* EIA sensitivity: -149 dB 150 ohm: -56 dB* EIA sensitivity: -150 dB 250 ohm: -56 dB* EIA sensitivity: -148 dB (*0 dB=l mw/10 dynes/cm2)
Polar Pattern:	Cardioid
Impedance:	50, 150, 250 ohms, connected for 150 ohms when shipped.
Hum Pickup Level:	-125 dBm ref: relative to 0.001 gauss field. Shielded transformer with special humbucking coil almost totally eliminates hum pickup when in vicinity of AC fields
Diaphragm:	Electro-Voice Acoustalloy®
Case Material:	Die cast aluminum
Dimensions:	1-11/16 inch maximum diameter, 7-11/16 inches long

(SOURCE: ELECTRO-VOICE)

AKG C 451/452

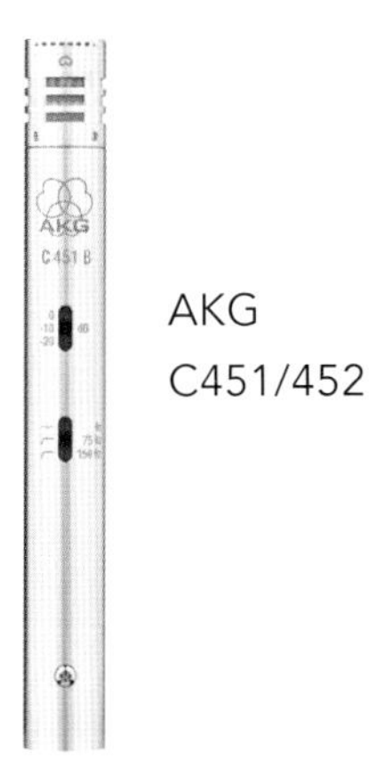

AKG C451/452

Operating Principle. Small-diaphragm condenser

Al's Preferred Applications. Hi-hat, snare top

A Note from Al. I use the 451 or 452 on the top of the snare drum and on the hi-hat. I aim the mic at the spot on the top of the snare where the drummer's sticks hit the head, and it gets a nice crisp sound. The 451 and 452 are basically the same microphone, but the 452 only works on 48V phantom power, and the 451 will work with phantom power or batteries.

Frequency Response and Polar Pattern

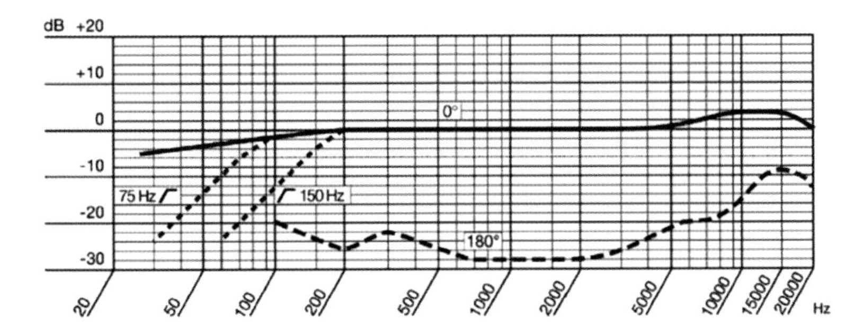

AKG C451

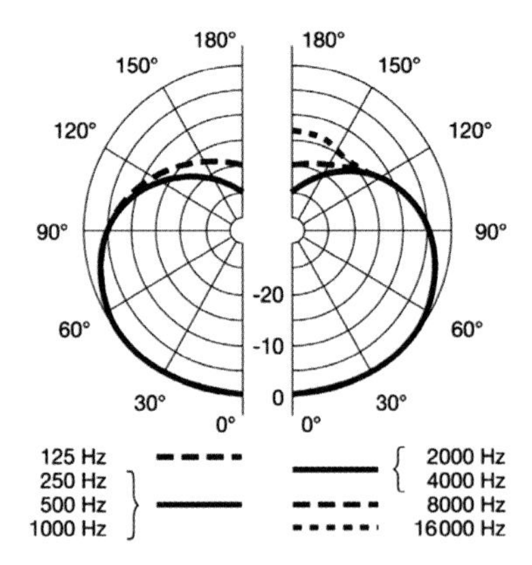

AKG C452

Technical Data

Transducer type	condenser
Frequency response	20 Hz–20 kHz
Sensitivity at 1 kHz	9 mV/Pa (-41 dB V)
Self noise level	18 dB-A
Dynamic range	117 dB
Polar pattern	cardioid
Impedance	200 ohms
Load impedance	>1000 ohms
Switchable pad	-10 and -20 dB
Sound pressure level for 0.5% THD	135 dB SPL (unpadded), 145 dB SPL (-10 dB pad), 155 dB SPL (-20 dB pad)
LF roll-off	12 dB/octave at 75 and 150 Hz
Power requirement	451 (9 to 52 Vdc), 452 48V phantom power)
Finish	Satin nickel
Size	.75 inches diameter (19 mm), 6.3 inches length (160 mm)

(SOURCE: HARMAN PROFESSIONAL)

AKG C12

AKG C12

Operating Principle. Large-diaphragm condenser (tube)

Al's Preferred Applications. Strings

A Note from Al. The first time I went to Columbia Studios in New York, "The Church," they had 15–20 C12s hanging all over the room. That was a big mic for Columbia. I think they used them on Johnny Mathis, and a lot of them were used on the Miles Davis recordings. The only time I used them was when I was at Columbia. I had a big string date with George Benson in The Church and the sound was great.

Note: CBS 30th Street Studio, operated by Columbia Records from 1949 to 1981 and located in Manhattan, New York City, was nicknamed "The Church." It was also mentioned just as 30th Street Studio, 30th Street Studios, and Columbia Recording Studios.

Frequency Response and Polar Pattern

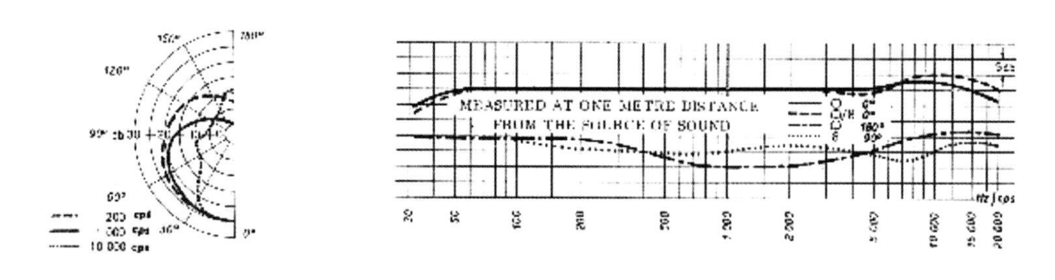

AKG C12 frequency response and polar pattern

Technical Data

Frequency Range	20–20,000 cps
Frequency Response	± 2 dB related to published curve
Directional Characteristics (nine different positions)	omnidirectional cardioid: better than 20 dB front-to-back ratio at 180° sound incidence bidirectional: 20 dB front-to-back ratio
Sensitivity	1.0 mV/μbar (–60 dB re 1 V/dyne/cm2), unloaded (200 ohms)
Equivalent Noise Level	less than 20 dB
Impedance	50/200 ohms (change solder lugs)
Tube Complement	1 x 6072, 6.3 volts DC filament voltage,
120 volts DC plate voltage	
Mains Connection	110/125/145/220/245 volts AC at 50/60 cps
Stand Connector	3⁄8", ½", 5⁄8"-27 with microphone cable MK 12
Dimensions	10" (255 mm) with connector, 11⁄16" diameter (43 mm)
Weight	1 lb. 3.2 oz. net (560 g), shipping weight 29 lbs. 12.8 oz. (13.5 kg)

(SOURCE: HARMAN PROFESSIONAL)

AKG C12A

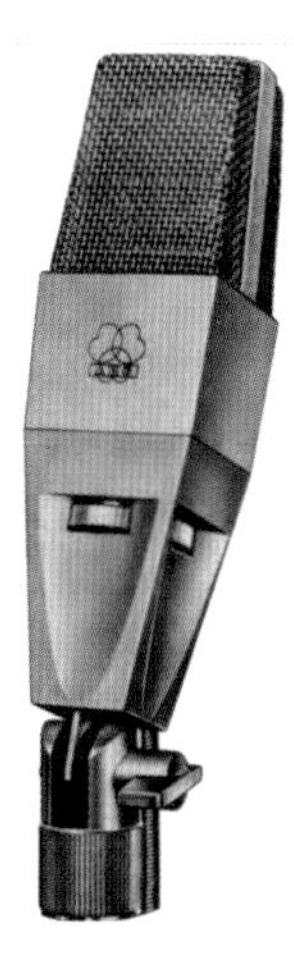

AKG C12A

Operating Principle. Large-diaphragm condenser (tube)

Al's Preferred Applications. Drum overheads, piano

A Note from Al. I have a couple C12As that came as a matched pair from the factory. I used to use them as drum overheads. There is quite a big difference between the C12 and the C12A. As much as they tried to make the newer C12A sound like the C12, it doesn't. The C12A just doesn't have the warmth that the C12 had. To me, the C12A is a little brighter at the top end and it doesn't have nice low end that the C12 has, but it's a very good choice for overheads.

Frequency Response and Polar Pattern

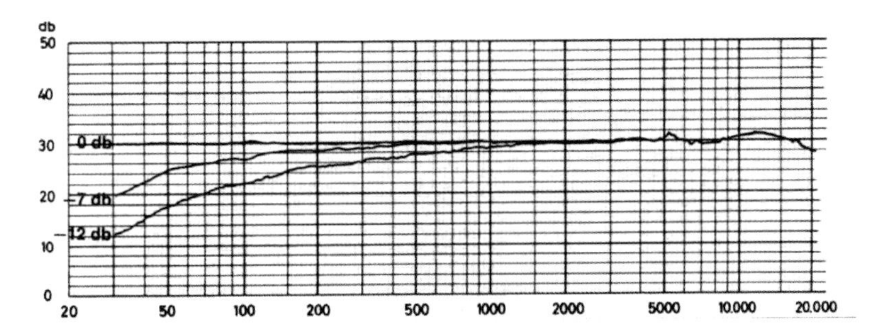

AKG C12A

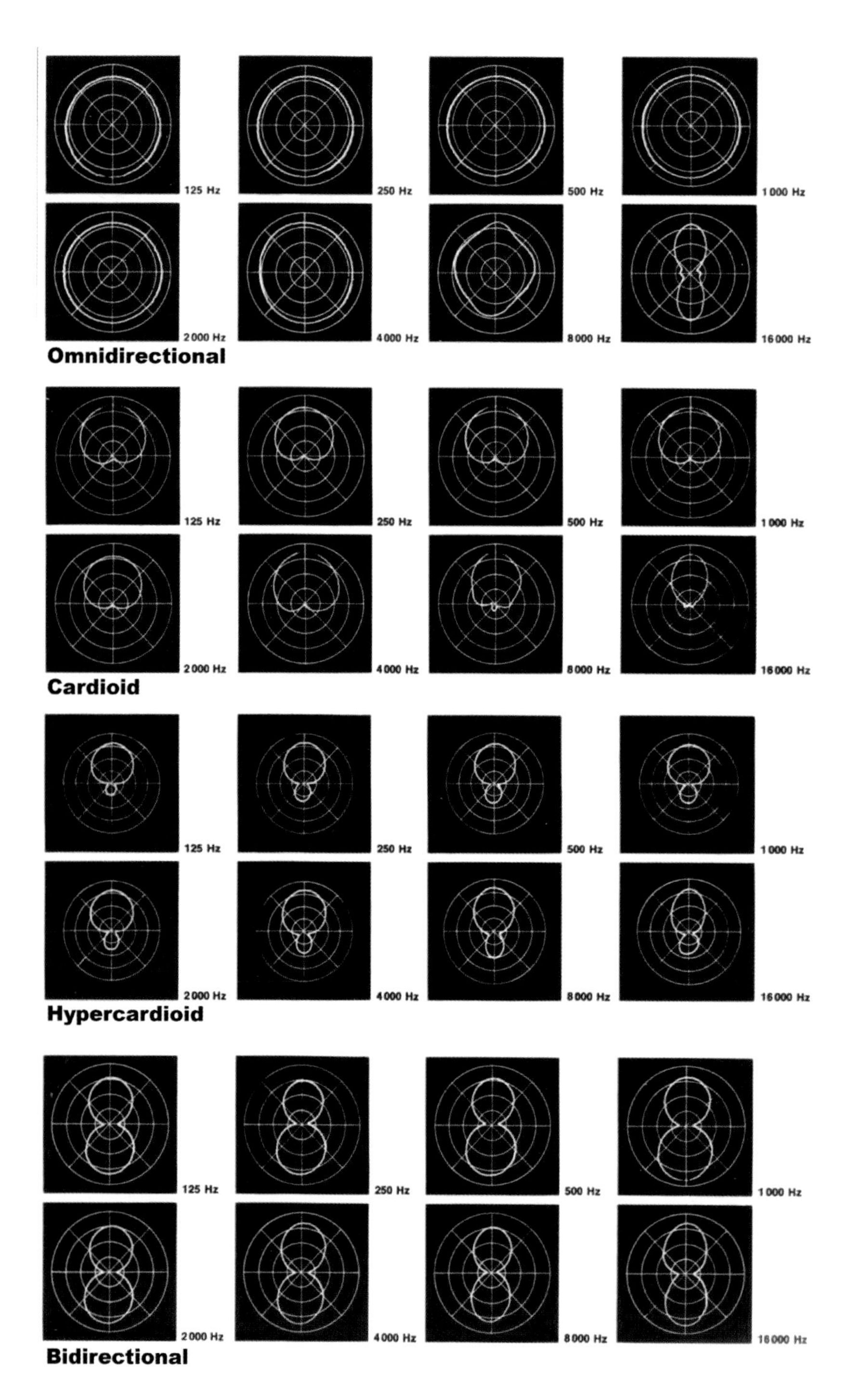

AKG C12A polar patterns (omnidirectional, wide, cardioid, hypercardioid, bidirectional)

Technical Data

Type	Pressure-gradient with low-frequency circuit and pattern selector
Frequency Range:	10–20,000 cps (related to published curve
Sensitivity at 1000 cps:	0.4 mv/ µbar (-68 dBv) re.1 v/dyne/cm2. Microphone rating: GM = -140 dB; -46 dB re.1 mw/10 dyne/cm2
Impedance (Min. Actual):	200 ohms + 15% (50 ohms, change solder lugs)
Load Impedance:	500 ohms (150 ohms)
Directional Characteristic:	Cardioid, omni-directional, figure-of-eight and 6 intermediate positions
Bass Switch:	0, -7, -12 dB (50 cps)
Weighted Noise Level:	0.6 µveff (Filter CCIF 1954 DIN 45 405)
Unweighted Noise Level:	2.0 µveff
Equivalent Noise Level:	Better than 20 dB SPL (Filter CCIF 1954 DIN 45 405)
Maximum Sound Pressure Level at a distortion of 0.5%:	40 cps ... 150 µbar (117.5 dB), 1000 cps ... 150 µbar (117.5 dB), 5000 cps ... 150 µbar (117.5 dB)
Sensitivity to Magnetic Stray Field:	At 50 cps: 0.02 v/s/m2 = 0.1 mv/50 mgauss
Capsule Capacity:	2x100pF
Plate Voltage:	120 V
Plate Current:	2.4 mA
Filament Voltage:	5.0 V ±5%
Filament Current:	122 mA
Temperature:	From -14° F to + 150° F (-10° C to + 60° C)
Tube:	7586 Nuvistor
Power Supply:	220, 110v ± 10°/0; 50/60cps

(SOURCE: HARMAN PROFESSIONAL)

AKG C12 VR

AKG
C12 VR

Operating Principle. Large-diaphragm condenser (tube)

Al's Preferred Applications. Trumpet (room), saxophone (room), drum overheads

A Note from Al. I have two C12 VRs and I use them as room mics for trumpets, saxophones, and sometimes drum overheads. They're great mics. They're expensive mics and they're well made. The frequency response is good. To compare it to another mic, the closest thing I can think of would be the Neumann M 149

Frequency Response and Polar Pattern

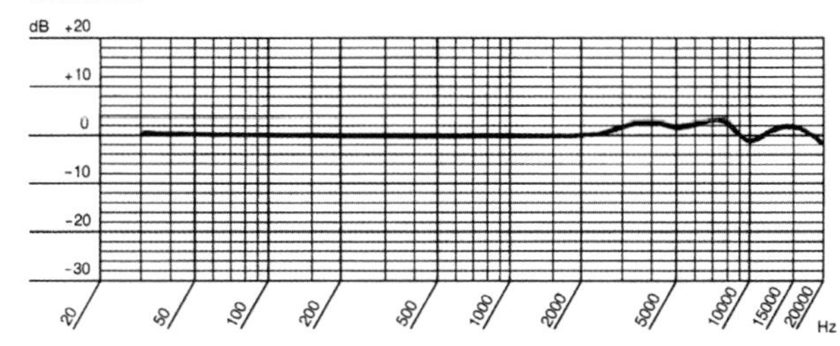

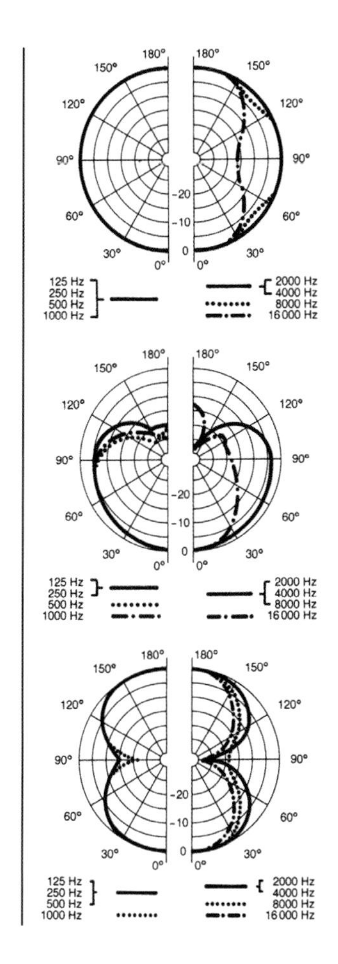

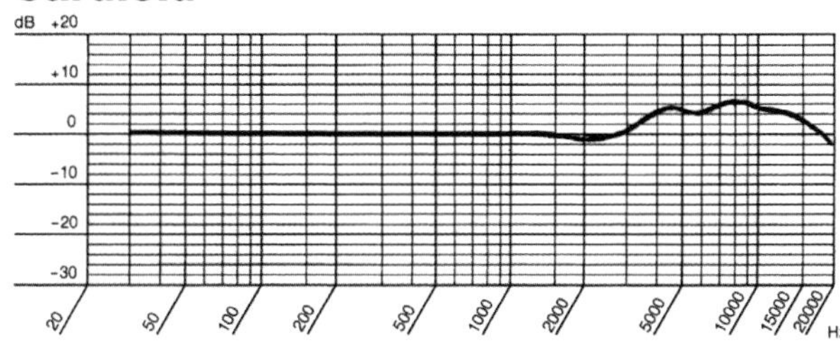

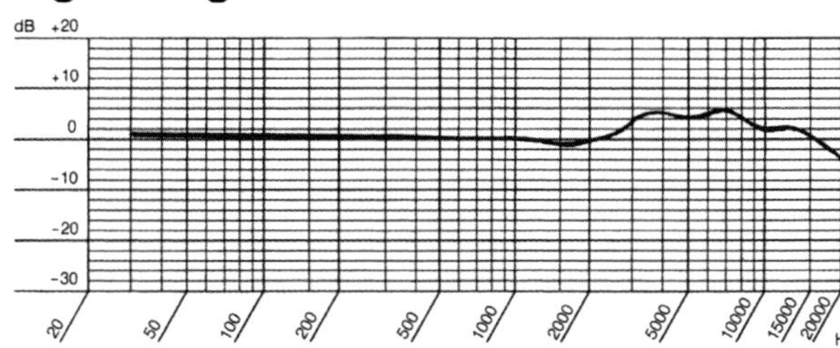

AKG C12 VR frequency response and polar pattern

Technical Data

Audio frequency bandwidth	30–20000 Hz
Equivalent noise level	22 dB-A
Sensitivity	10 mV/Pa
Signal to Noise	72 dB-A
Preattenuation	Pad-10; -20 dB
Bass cut filter	100; 130 Hz
Electrical impedance	200 Ohms
Recommended load impedance	1000 Ohms
Polar Patterns	Cardioid, omnidirectional, and figure-of-eight

(SOURCE: HARMAN PROFESSIONAL)

AKG C 414

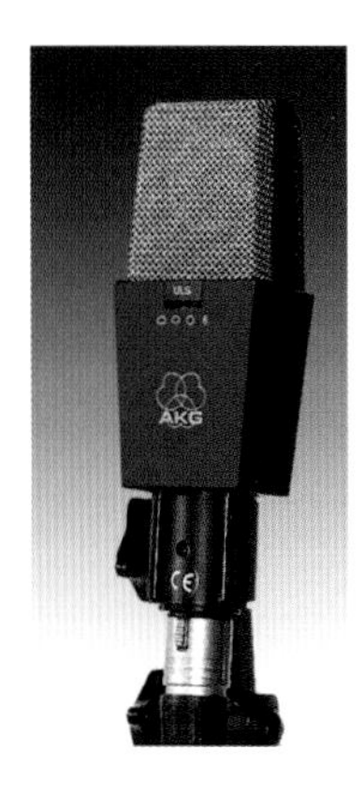

AKG C 414
(PHOTO BY STANLEY COUTANT)

Operating Principle. Large-diaphragm condenser

Al's Preferred Applications. Toms, percussion table, piano, timbales

A Note from Al. I like the sound of the 414 on toms. Sometimes I'll use it on percussion and it'll work fine on piano, but I use my M 149s now. I use them on timbales, too. I put one up, level with the percussionist's head, and one aimed at the side of the timbale because the players hit the side a lot. That's pretty much what I use them for now, but the 414 is a very nice microphone. It's the crispness in the high end that I like a lot. In fact, I used a 414 on Jackson Browne for lead vocal back in the '80s. It sounded good. There were a few people trying the 414 on vocals at that time.

Frequency Response and Polar Pattern

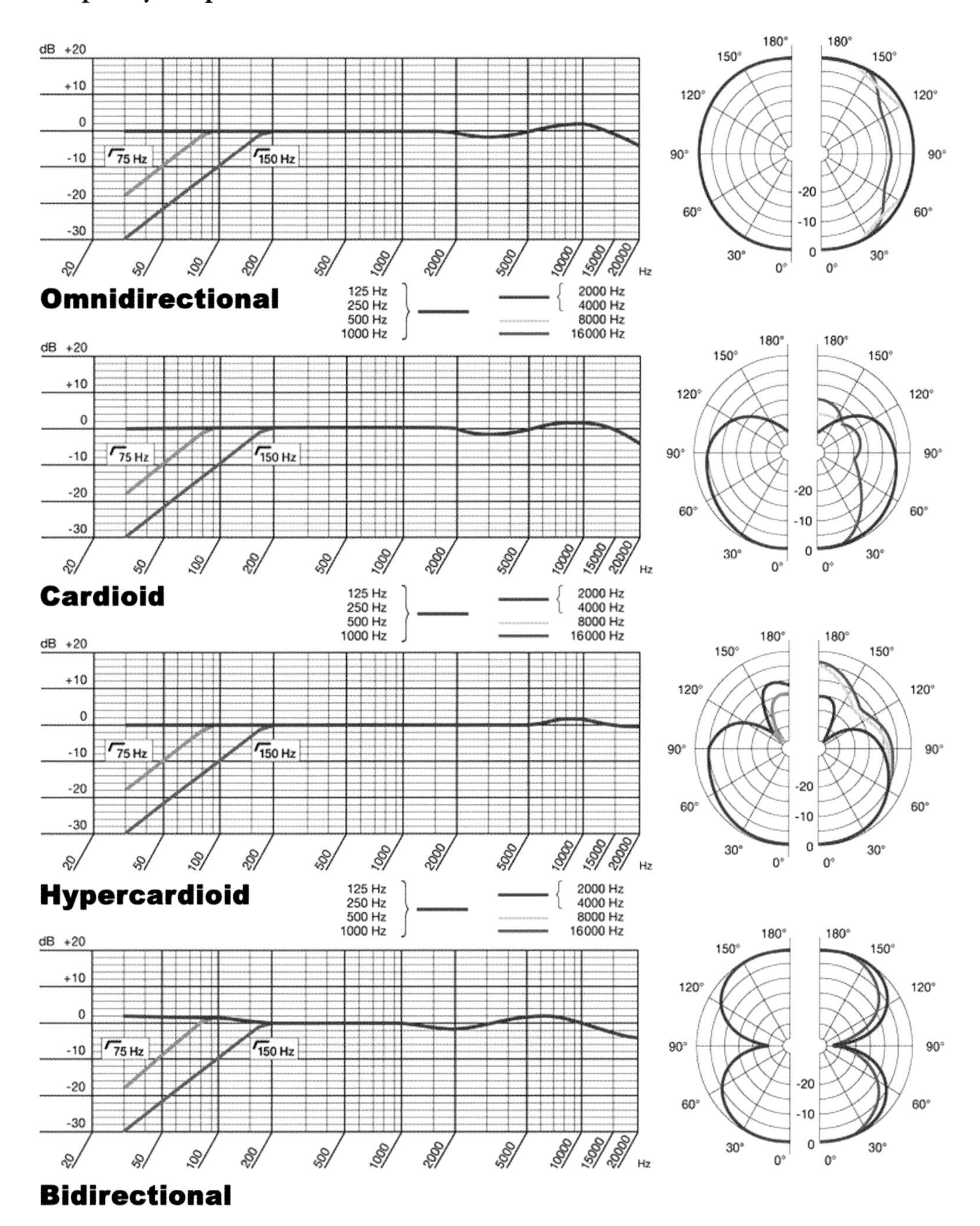

AKG C414 frequency response and polar patterns (cardioid, hypercardiold, omnidirectional, bidirectional)

Technical Data

Polar pattern	cardioid, hypercardiold, omnidirectional, figure-eight
Frequency range Sensitivity	20–20,000 Hz
Max. SPL	12.5 mV/Pa (-38 dBV)
Equivalent noise level (CCIR 468-3)	140/150/160 dB (THD=0.5%)
Equivalent noise level	25 dB
Signal/noise ratio	14 dB-A
(A-weighted)	14 dB-A
Preattenuation pad	10 dB, 20 dB, selectable
Bass filter	12 dB/octave at 75 or 150 Hz
Impedance	180 ohms
Recommended load Impedance	>1000 ohms
Supply voltage	9 to 52 V phantom power to DIN 45596
Current consumption	<2 mA
Connector	3-pln XLR
Finish	matte black/sliver
Dimensions	141 x45 x 35 mm / 5.6 x 1.8 x 1.4 In.
Net weight	320 g / 11.3 oz.

(SOURCE: HARMAN PROFESSIONAL)

AKG D12

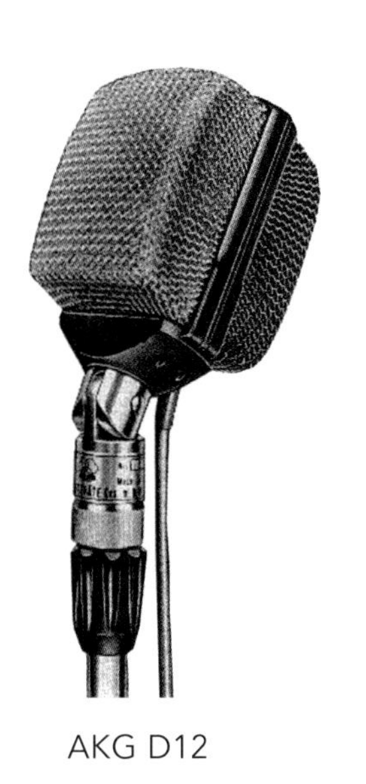

AKG D12

Insensitive to sound reaching this dynamic microphone from the rear...An exceptionally pronounced cardioid pattern produces an acoustical shield of approximately 180° that effectively isolates unwanted sounds originating from noisy audiences, feed-back or reflection.

Vintage AKG D12 flyer

Operating Principle. Dynamic

Al's Preferred Applications. Kick drum

A Note from Al. A friend of mine from Germany came over and gave me a gift, which was the fourth D12 ever made! Before that, I had been using the D112 on the kick all the time, but then I got the D12 and I fell in love with it. I love the sound of it, and I also really love the fact that it was the fourth one they made. Both the D12 and D112 work great on the kick, but that's really all I'd ever use those mics on.

The D112 is probably a little brighter than the D12 but I really like the low end of the D 12. It has more of the thump that I like.

Frequency Response and Polar Pattern

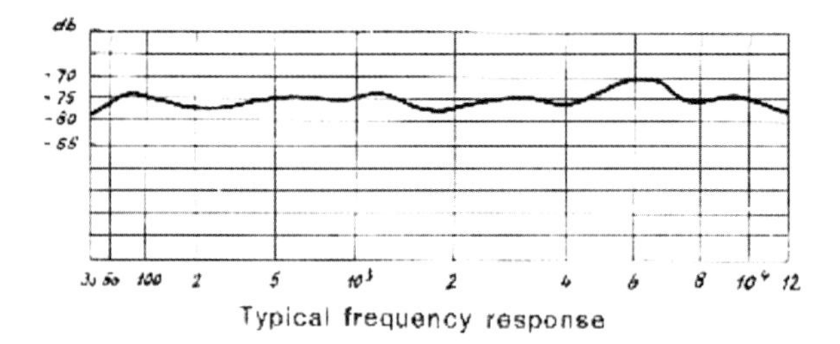

AKG D12 frequency response

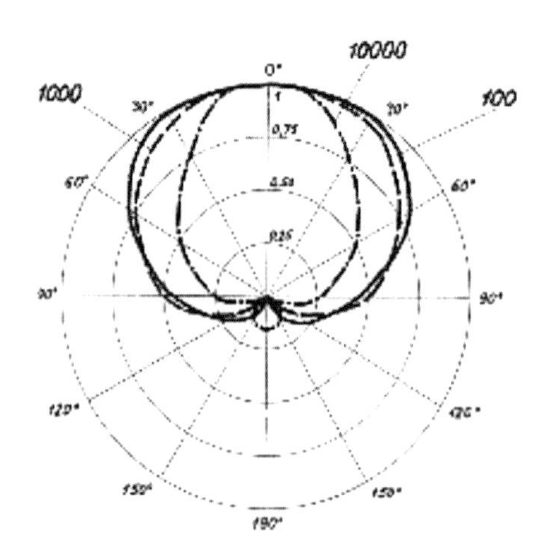

AKG D12 polar pattern

Technical Data

Frequency range	40–15,000 cps
Frequency response	± 3 DB related to published curve
Directional characteristic	cardioid
Front to back ratio	approximately 18 dB at 180-degree sound incidence
Impedance	200 ohms, if specified 60 ohms
Sensitivity, unloaded	0.16 mV/µbar (-77 dB re 1 v/dyne/cm2)

(SOURCE: HARMAN PROFESSIONAL)

Shure SM57

Shure SM57

Operating Principle. Dynamic

Al's Preferred Applications. Under snare, guitar amp

A Note from Al. I use the 57 on the bottom of the snare drum. I get it as close to the snares as I can and then invert the phase so that it works together with the top snare mic. That works really well for me.

The SM57 is a good go-to mic if you're doing a live show or that kind of thing, because it'll take a real beating and just keep working. There have been a lot of great recordings made with just that microphone. I know that Niko Bolas just did something recently in Nashville, and he used nothing but 57s on everything, and it sounded amazing. He just wanted to see if he could do it, and really, it just sounded incredible

If I'm in a studio, and I don't have my go-to mics, I'll use an SM57 on the guitar amps. I used to use nothing but 57s on guitar amps. That's what I was using on Steve Lukather when we did the Toto recordings. Then when newer mics came out that I liked better, I started switching. The other mics that I like on guitar now are the Royer-122 and the AT4080. There's a smoother quality to these newer ribbon mics that I like a lot. I think they give me more of what I'm getting out of the amplifier.

Technical Data

Type	Dynamic
Frequency Response	40–15,000 Hz
Polar Pattern	Cardioid
Sensitivity (at 1,000 Hz Open Circuit Voltage)	Open Circuit Voltage: -56.0 dBV/Pa (1.6 mV) (1 Pa = 94 dB SPL)
Impedance	Rated impedance is 150Ω (310Ω actual) for connection to microphone inputs rated low impedance.
Polarity	Positive pressure on diaphragm produces positive voltage on pin 2 with respect to pin 3.
Case	Dark gray, enamel-painted, die-cast steel with a polycarbonate grille and a stainless-steel screen.
Connector	Three-pin professional audio connector (male XLR type)
Net Weight	284 grams (10 oz.)
Dimensions	157 mm (6-3/16 in.) L x 32 mm (1-1/4 in.) W at the widest point

(SOURCE: SHURE INCORPORATED)

Frequency Response and Polar Pattern

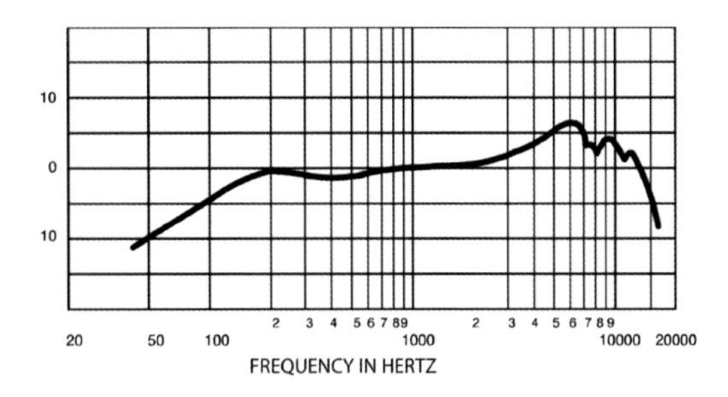

Shure SM57 frequency response

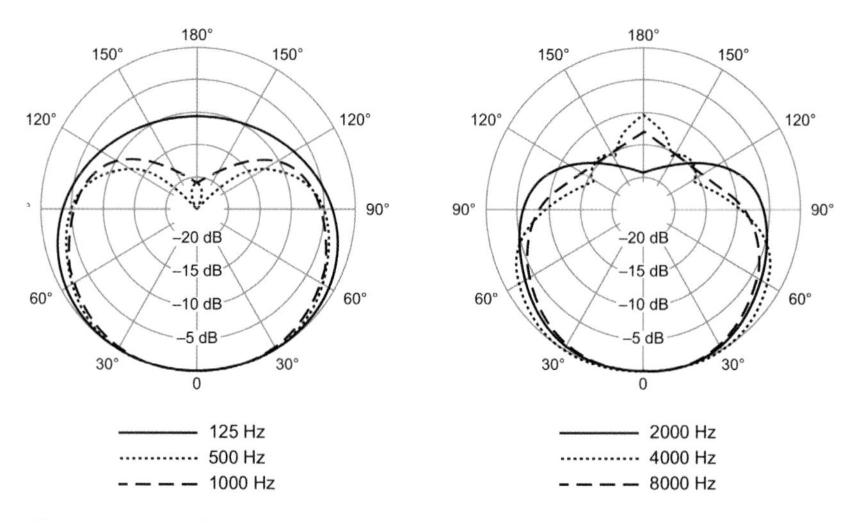

Shure SM57 polar pattern

RCA 77-DX

RCA 77-DX
(PHOTO BY STANLEY COUTANT)

Operating Principle. Ribbon

Al's Preferred Applications. Upright piano, chimes, solo trumpet, vocal (vintage)

A Note from Al. I used to use the 77 for upright piano, chimes, solo trumpet, and even vocals. It was a great go-to mic. Before we had windscreens, we taped a pencil to the front of the microphone in front of the ribbon to block the wind from the singers plosives. It was an amazingly good ribbon mic. And it had three switches, so you could change the sound. I used to use it all the time on brass before we had some of the great options we have now.

I'd still use it on a solo trumpet or something like that. Most of the players now, though, ask for the Royer. The biggest problem with the older ribbon mic is finding one with a ribbon that's in good shape. The ribbons can get worn down or damaged, and then you lose the frequency response, and you can't really use it. But if you have one that's in great shape and has been taken care, they're great-sounding mics.

Technical Data

Output Impedance	250 ohms may be changed to 30 or 150 ohms
Load Impedance	Unloaded input transformer
Effective Output Level (all output connections)	Bi-directional (B) -50 dBm Gm= -144 dB Uni-directional (U) -53 dBm Gm= -147 dB Non-directional (N) -56 dBm Gm= -150 dB L-1, L-2, L-3, between -50 and -53 dBm (Gm = RTMA rating)
Hum Pick-up Level	-128 dBm
Dimensions and Weight	Length: S1 l½ inches Width: 3½ inches Depth: 2½ inches Weight: Total 4½ pounds Cable Less cable 3 pounds
Cable	MI-43-D, 3-conductor, shielded, 30 feet long, no plug
Finish	TV Gray and satin chrome (MI-4045-F) TV Gray (MI-11006-C)
Stand Fitting	½-inch pipe thread

(SOURCE: STANLEY COUTANT, WWW.COUTANT.ORG)

Frequency Response and Polar Pattern

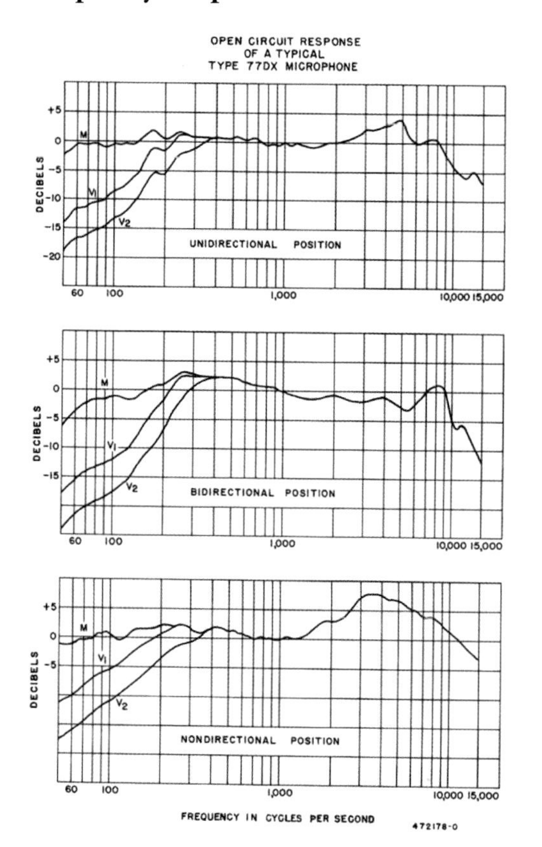

RCA 77-DX frequency response
(FROM STANLEY COUTANT)

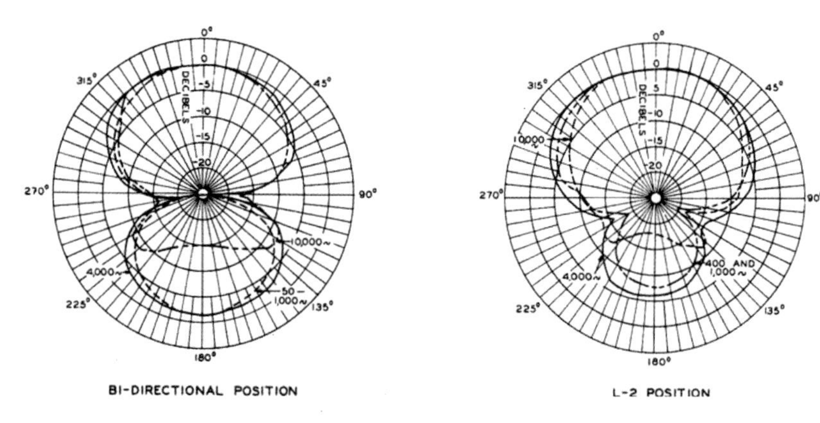

RCA 77-DX polar pattern (FROM STANLEY COUTANT)

RCA 44-BX

RCA 44-BX
(PHOTO BY STANLEY COUTANT)

Operating Principle. Ribbon

Al's Preferred Applications. Vocal duet, choir

A Note from Al. The RCA 44 is another great-sounding mic. It's one of the best microphones for background vocalists and for choirs. That's all we used to use for those. When we did all those Ray Charles records with Betty Carter with the choir, and we did a country western record with him too, we set up four 44s and we put four people on each mic—two on one side and two on the other, and we had them lined up. We always did it that way if we had 12 or 16 singers in the choir. All the Elvis Presley records we did with the background singers were all done using 44s.

I don't use those mics at all anymore. If I had to come up with an old-fashion sound, I might bring those mics out, but that's about it.

Frequency Response and Polar Pattern

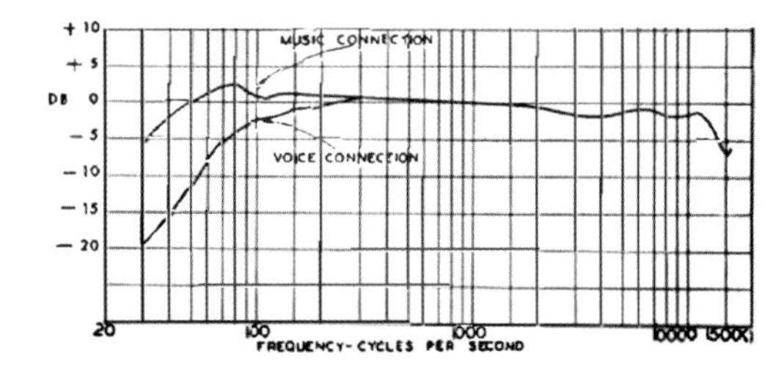

RCA 44-BX frequency response
(FROM STANLEY COUTANT)

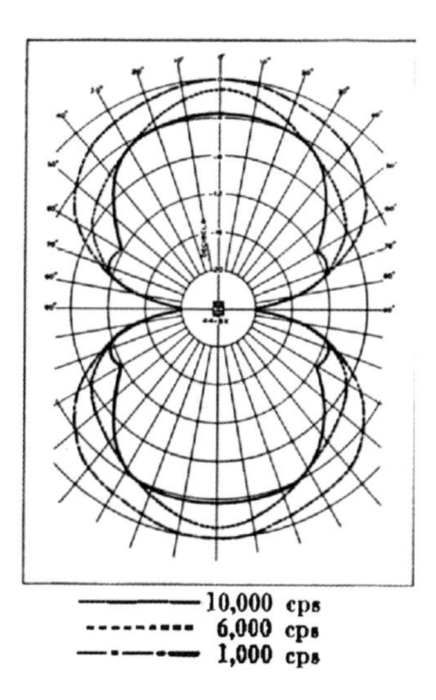

RCA 44-BX polar pattern
(FROM STANLEY COUTANT)

Technical Data

Directional characteristic	Bidirectional
Output impedance	30/150/250 ohms
Effective output level	-55 dBm*
Hum pickup level	112 dBm**
Frequency response	50–15,000 cycles
Finish	Umber gray and satin chrome
Mounting	½-inch pipe
Dimensions, overall Height (including cushion mounting Width Depth	 12inches 4 ¾ inches 3 3/8 inches
Weight (unpacked including mountings	8 ½ lbs.
Cable (MI-43 A) 3-conductor shielded	30 feet (no plug)
*Referred to 0.001 watt and a sound pressure of 10 dynes/cm3 (94 dB level) **Referred to 0.001 watt and a 60 cycle hum field of 0.001 gauss	

(SOURCE: STANLEY COUTANT, WWW.COUTANT.ORG)

Royer R-122 MkII/122v

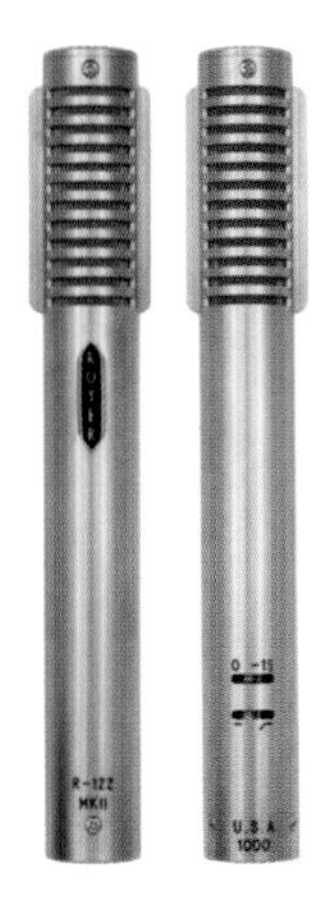

Royer R-122 active ribbon microphone

Operating Principle. Ribbon (active)

Al's Preferred Applications. Bass amp, acoustic guitar, guitar amp, trombone

A Note from Al. I probably end up using the Royer R-122 and the 122v the most out of the Royer mics that I have, but they're all great microphones. I use them on the guitar amp a lot, and even acoustic guitar at times. And they're great on trombones. I'll use four of them in a big band session—one on each of the trombones, about a foot and a half in front of the bells.

Frequency Response and Polar Pattern (R-122)

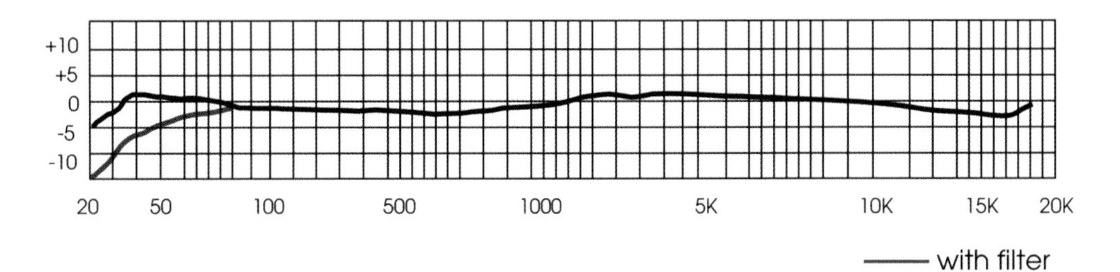

Royer R-122 frequency response

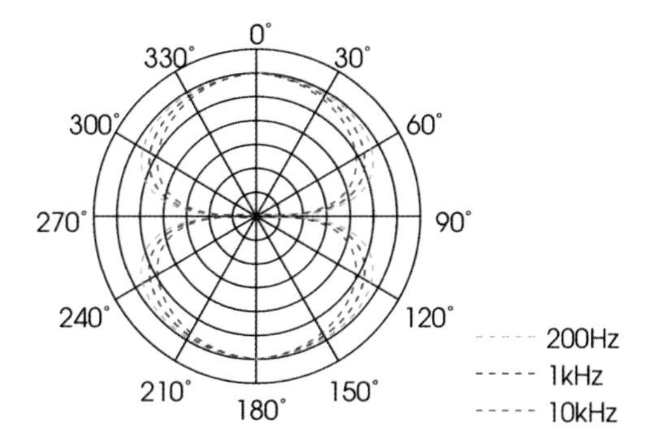

Royer R-122 polar pattern

Technical Data (R-122)

Acoustic Operating Principle	Electrodynamic pressure gradient with active electronics.
Polar Pattern	Figure-8
Generating Element	2.5-micron aluminum ribbon
Magnets	Rare Earth Neodymium
Frequency Response	30–15,000 Hz ±3 dB
Sensitivity	-36 dB (re. 1v/pa ±1 dB)
Switchable Pad	-15 dB
Switchable Bass Cut	100 Hz (6 dB per octave)
Self-Noise	< 18 dB
Output Impedance	200 Ohms, balanced
Output Connector	Male XLR 3-pin (Pin 2 Hot)
Rated Load Impedance	1 kOhm minimum
Maximum SPL	135 dB @ 30 Hz
Power Requirements	48-Volt Phantom Only
Supply Current	4 mA
Dimensions	206mm L X 25mm W (8 1/8" L X 1" W)
Weight	309 grams (10.9 oz)
Finish	Burnished Satin Nickel/Matte Black Chrome (optional)

(SOURCE: ROYER LABS MICROPHONES)

Royer SF-24

Royer SF-24
active stereo
ribbon microphone

Operating Principle. Active stereo ribbon

Al's Preferred Applications. Over conductor for orchestra, drum overhead, piano room mic

A Note from Al. I love the SF-24 Royer stereo mic! I put it up over the conductor for some sessions, and it just sounds great. Royer just keeps making their mics better and better. I have a couple of the SF-1s and the first stereo Royer, the SF-12, and I like those mics, but they keep getting better. Right now I use the 122, 122v (the tube model), and the SF-24 the most.

Frequency Response and Polar Pattern

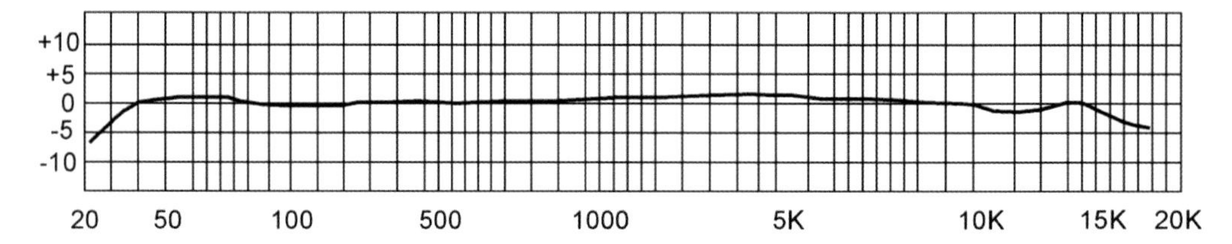

Royer SF-24 frequency response

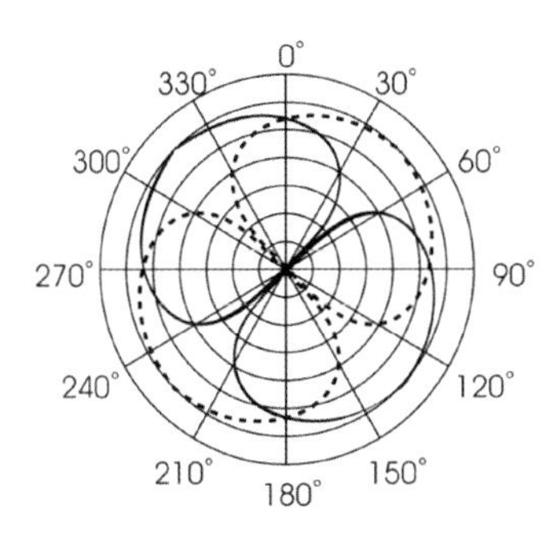

Royer SF-24 polar pattern

Technical Data

Acoustic Operating Principle:	Electro-dynamic pressure gradient with active electronics
Polar Pattern:	Symmetrical Figure-8
Generating Elements:	Two 1.8-micron aluminum ribbons
Frequency Response:	30 Hz–15,000 Hz ± 3 dB
Sensitivity	>-38 dBv Ref 1 v/pa
Self Noise:	<18 dB
Output Impedance	300 ohms @ I kHz
Recommended Load Impedance:	>1500 ohms
Maximum SPL:	>130 dB
Output Connector:	Male XLR 5-pin
Power Requirements:	48-Volt Phantom (per channel) only
Supply Current:	4 mA per channel
Dimensions	270 mm X 39 mm (base) X 25 mm (top) (10 5/8" X 1.5"qq wide (base) X 1" wide (top))
Weight	531 grams (18.7 ounces)
Finish	Optical Black Chrome 18K Gold (optional)

(SOURCE: ROYER LABS MICROPHONES)

Mojave MA-300

Mojave MA-300

Operating Principle. Large-diaphragm condenser (tube)

Al's Preferred Applications. Sax

A Note from Al. When I can't get the U 67s, I use the Mojave MA-300s on saxes. The MA-300 is a great-sounding microphone, and it has a reasonable price. It has a sound that's similar to the Neumann U 67. It might sound good on some of the other things I like to use the U 67 for, but I haven't had the opportunity to try because I have a pretty well-established group of mics that I use. I do like the MA-300 a lot on sax though. I have five of them, and I love the way they sound.

Frequency Response and Polar Pattern

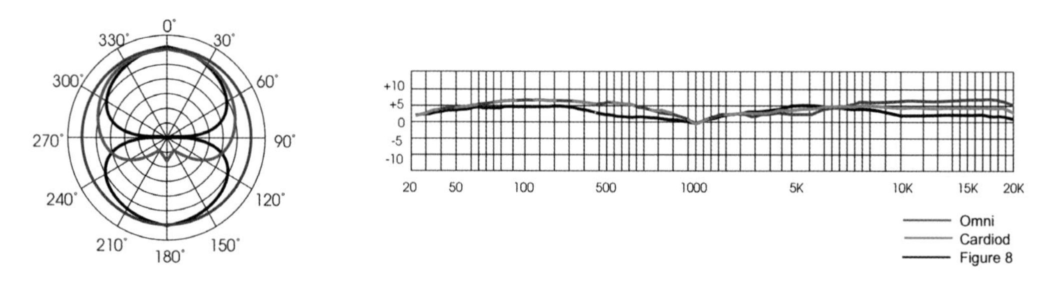

Mojave MA-300 frequency response and polar pattern

Technical Data

Transducer Type	Externally polarized, pressure gradient capacitor - double diaphragm.
Diaphragm	1-inch diameter, gold sputtered
Diaphragm thickness	3 microns
Polar Pattern	Continuously variable from omnidirectional to figure-eight.
Frequency response	20 Hz–20 KHZ, ±3 dB at "flat" setting of bass cut switch. Bass cut switch provides 6 dB per octave attenuation below 100 Hertz in "cut" setting
Sensitivity	-37dB, re. 1V/pa
Maximum SPL	120 dB with pad off, 135 dB with pad on
Distortion	< 1% @ 117 dB SPL, < 3% @ 125 dB SPL with pad off < 1% @ 132 dB SPL, < 3% @ 140 dB SPL with pad on
Self noise	14 dB nominal, not to exceed 16 dB A-weighted
Pad	15 dB
Bass cut	6 dB per octave below 100 Hz
Dimensions and weight	Carrying case with microphone, power supply, shock mount and cables: 13 lbs. (5.9Kg) Microphone: 7 5/8" X 2" (194mm x 51mm), 1 lb. (0.45Kg)

RCA Type KU-3A (also known as the "10001")

RCA Type KU-3A (also known as the "10001") (PHOTO BY STANLEY COUTANT)

Operating Principle. Ribbon

Al's Preferred Applications. Trombones, French horns

A Note from Al. Wow, what a great microphone. On all the Mancini dates, that's all I used on trombone. It's just an amazing microphone. Unfortunately, the only place I know that has any of them is the Warner Brothers Clint Eastwood scoring stage. They have about 12 of them. It's an RCA mic, so when I was working at RCA, we had plenty of them, so I used them a lot. They're like a 44, but one-sided and cardioid. There was a warmth to them that was amazing. They were perfect for trombones and French horns. You don't really see them anymore, and if you do, somebody might have just one.

Frequency Response and Polar Pattern

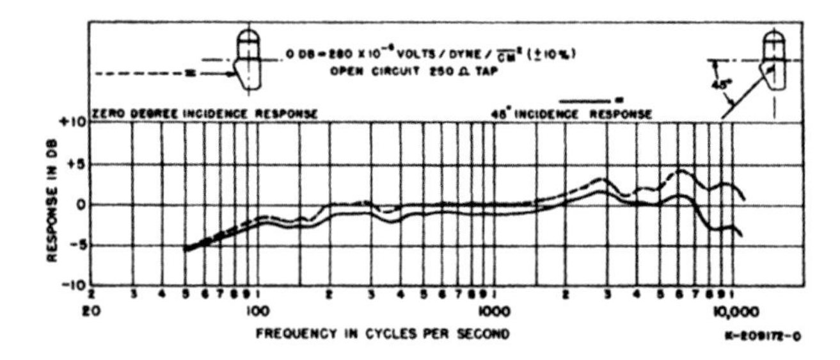

RCA KU-3A frequency response

(FROM STANLEY COUTANT)

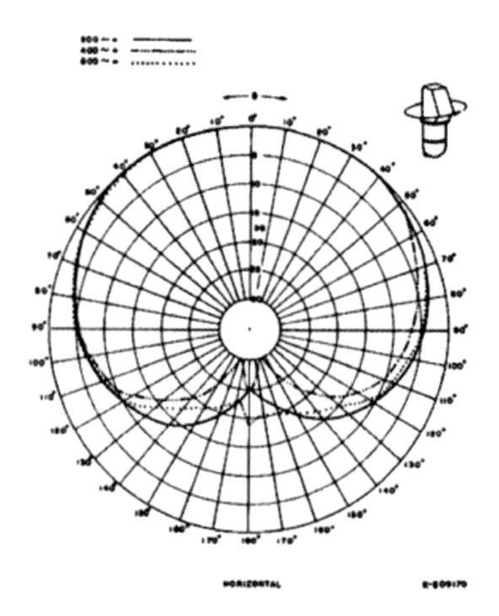

RCA KU-3A polar pattern

(FROM STANLEY COUTANT)

Technical Data

Output impedance	30, 150, 250 ohms (connected for 250 ohms when shipped)
Load impedance	Open circuit (unterminated transformer)
Effective output level at 1000 Hz (10 dynes/cm2 input)	-49 dBm at 30 ohms, -51 dBm at 150 and 250 ohms
Frequency response	30–15,000 Hz
Directional characteristic	Cardioid
External connection	12-inch long "pigtail" without plug
Finish	Flat two-tone umber gray
Dimensions	Length 8", width 3", depth 3 1/2" (20.32 cm, 7.62 cm, 8.89 cm)
Weight (less suspension mounting)	2 lbs. 13 oz. (1.25 kg.)

PREAMPS AND EQS

Cinema EQ 4031-B

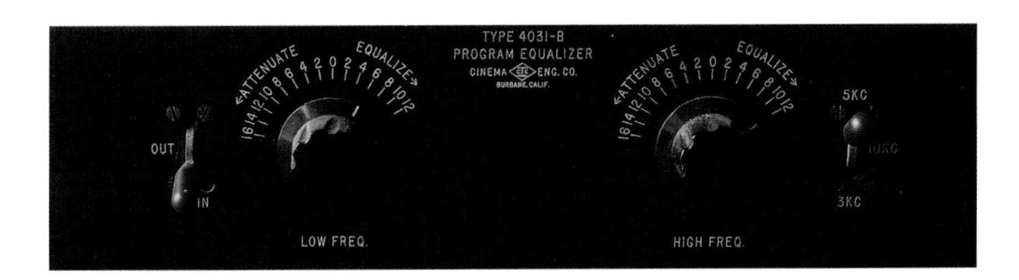

Cinema Engineering 4031-B

Al's Preferred Application. Program equalizer

A Note from Al. When I started, we only had six or eight inputs on the board, so all you could use was six or eight microphones. There was no mixing. We were going directly to disc, or later directly to mono tape. The Cinema equalizer was the only EQ at that time, and if you used it, you had to equalize everything—the entire mono mix. You couldn't just patch it in on the bass or just on the vocal. You had to equalize everything, so we didn't really use it very often.

But we did really care about the sounds we were getting, and we had to rely on choosing the right mics, and using them in the way that captured the sound we wanted for the recording. It was a great way to learn, because we found out quickly that just moving the mic a couple of inches made a big difference in the sound of the instrument you were capturing. It was an incredible way to learn, and I was blessed to have great mentors like Tommy Dowd and Bob Daugherty.

The EQ itself had one side that you could boost 3K, 5K, and 10K, and the other side where you could cut the low end.

Technical Data

Circuit	Bridged "T" type. (constant impedance)
Impedance	500–600 ohms only (unbalanced). For other impedances use separate transformers. Matching networks may be used.
Insertion loss	14 dB. (A fixed attenuator pad maintains insertion loss when switching in or out of program lines).
Input level	Minimum -70 dBm. Maximum +20 dBm.
Controls	Independent high and low frequency controls adjustable in 2-dB steps provide 12-dB equalization and 16-dB attenuation for both ends of the audio spectrum. A key at the right of the high frequency control knob allows for setting the high frequency equalization peak at either 3 KC, 5 KC, or 10 KC. This key does not influence the high frequency attenuation which always remains in steps of 2 dB at 10 KC. A key at the left of the low frequency control knob provides for switching the entire equalizer "'in" or "out". (Key automatically compensates for insertion loss when in the "out" position).
Power requirements	None.
Mounting	Standard RTMA rack mounting.
Panel finish	Cinema Grey baked enamel.
Dimensions	3½" x 19", depth behind panel 51/.1 ".
Net weight	12 lbs.
Shipping weight	16 lbs.

Neve 1073 and 1081 Preamp/EQ

Neve 1073

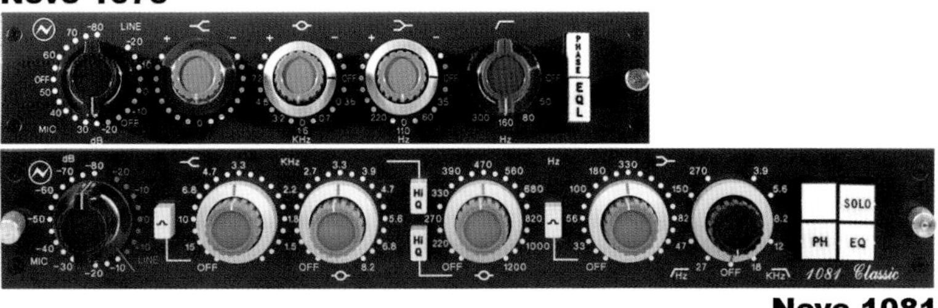

Neve 1081

Vintage Neve 1073 and 1081. Launched in 1970, the Neve 1073 has been used on some of the most famous recordings of the past 40 years. Designed in 1972, the Neve 1081 was originally conceived as a combined mic/line preamp and equalizer section for the Neve modular consoles.

Al's Preferred Application. Drum mics (1073), vocals (1073), room mics (1081), guitar amp (1081)

Al's Commentary. The 1073 is a piece of equipment that is made really well and it can take a beating and still work. In the low end it gives me the punch that I want from a preamp. I use it a lot on certain instruments. I really like it on the drums, and I'll use one 1073 for each mic on the drums. If there are eight mics, we'll use eight 1073s. They sound great.

The 1081s are also great preamps. They sound a lot like the 1073s. The reason I've used all 1073s on the drums is because I've had access to more of them. I wouldn't want to mix the 1073s and 1081s with a few 1073s and a few1081s. To me that wouldn't be right.

I've only had a couple 1081s, and I would use them for things like room mics or for guitar amps. The 1073 and 1081 are close to the same. Honestly, I probably couldn't tell them apart in a blindfold test because they're so similar.

Technical Data 1073

Microphone Input Gain	+80 dB to +20 dB in 5-dB steps.
Line Input Impedance	10K ohms, gain +20 dB to -10 dB in 5dB-steps.
Output	Transformer balanced and earth free
Maximum output	>+26 dBu into 600 Ω.
Distortion	Not more than 0.07% from 50Hz to 10kHz at 20dBu output
Output impedance	(80kHz bandwidth) into 600 Ω.
Frequency Response	±0.5dB 20 Hz to 20 kHz, -3dB at 40 kHz. EQ Out.

Technical Data 1081

Microphone input gain	+80 dB to +10 dB in 5dB steps
Line input gain	+20 dB to -10 dB in 5 dB steps
Maximum output	>+26 dBu into 600 Ω; output impedance 75 Ω @1 kHz
Distortion	Not more than 0.07% at +20 dBu output
Frequency response	±0.5 dB 20 Hz–20 kHz, -3 dB at 45 kHz. EQ Out.
Output noise	Better than -80 dB at all line levels

Martinsound Martech MSS-10 preamp

Martinsound Martech MSS-10 preamp

Al's Preferred Application. Vocals

A Note from Al. The MSS-10 looks like a Telefunken power supply. I haven't used it in a while, but I was using it on vocals for quite a long time. When I first got it, I used it all the time.

It had a warmth to it that I really liked. Now I'll get an occasional call from somebody who wants to use it. In fact, Lady Gaga recently called and borrowed one of mine for something she was doing.

Another preamp that's really great is the Mastering Lab preamp that Doug Sax came up with. I have four of them, and I use them on trumpets all the time. If I don't have any trumpets, I'll use them on French horns. Those are beautiful. They were custom made and I think that's the only one he made. I don't think there's a model number or anything. They were fabulous, and they could handle a lot of level. If you went out into the studio to listen and then came back into the control room, you were hearing the same thing.

Technical Data

Gain	20 dB–65 dB
Maximum Input	+22.5 dBu (@ 1 kHz, THD 0.003%, 20 dB pad in)
Maximum Output	+24 dBu
Input Impedance	2,450 Ohms (@ 1 kHz)
Output Impedance	50 Ohms
Frequency Response	10 Hz–20 kHz (+0.5/-0.0)
EIN -126.5 dBu Typ.	(10 Hz–20 kHz, 150 Ohm Source)
THD+N 0.0015%	(20 dB Gain @ 1 kHz, +4 dBu Out)
CMRR	65 dB Gain 60 Hz 108 dB 1 kHz 85 dB 10k Hz 65 dB

Line driver section Gain	10 dB
Maximum Input	+24 dBu
Maximum Output	+24 dBu
Input Impedance	20k Ohms (Balanced)
Output Impedance	50 Ohms
Frequency Response	10 Hz–200 kHz (+0.0/-0.25)
THD+N	0.001% (0 dB Gain @ 1 kHz, +4 dBu Out)

Studer D19 MicVALVE preamp

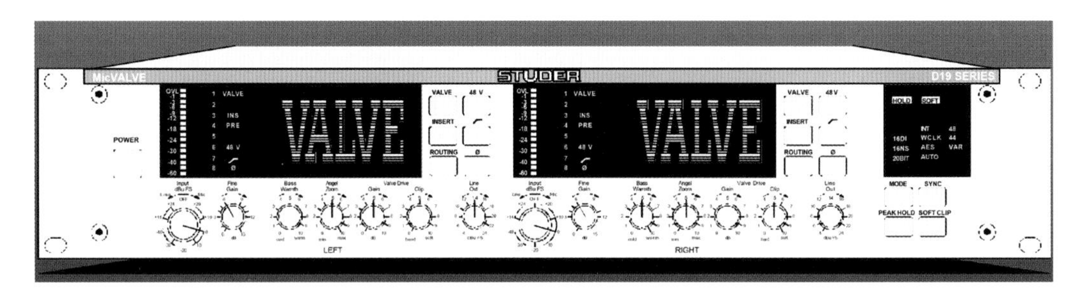

Studer D19 MicVALVE preamp

Al's Preferred Application. Trombones

A Note fromAl. I have four of the Studer MicValve preamps. I use them on trombones. I like those a lot. You can vary how much tube you use, or sometimes we won't use any tube. They're very versatile that way. They're great preamps.

I'm not the kind of engineer who likes to overdrive the preamp inputs for effect. I set my levels so the signal is pretty conservative. I might set the levels so the signal gets into the red a couple time, but that's about it. Somebody told me a long time ago that there's a reason there's an area of the meters that are red, and it's not good. So stay out of the red.

Even when we were on tape, my levels were correct. Some guys would send a lot of level to the tape to get away from the noise floor, but I didn't do that. It was better when we got Dolby because it controlled the noise. Really, though, one of the things people were missing when digital first came out was the hiss from the tape. After a while, our brain kind of nulled out the noise.

Technical Data

Frequency response	±0.15 dB
Signal/noise ratio	> 118 dBFS, CCIR 468-3
THD + Noise	< –80 dBFS, @ –1 dBFS, < –112 dBFS, @ –30 dBFS, Output Gain 24 dBuFS, < –103 dBFS, @ –30 dBFS, Output Gain 4 dBuFS
Crosstalk	< –100 dB, @ 15 kHz, Output Gain 24 dBuFS
Phase error	< ±1°
Insert:	Max. output level SEND: 17.2 dBuFS. Max. input level RETURN: 17.2 dBuFS
Microphone input impedance	1 kW
Line input impedance	11 kW
Insert Return	11 kW
Line output	< 20 W
Insert Send	50 W

COMPRESSORS

Fairchild 660 (mono)/670 (stereo) compressor

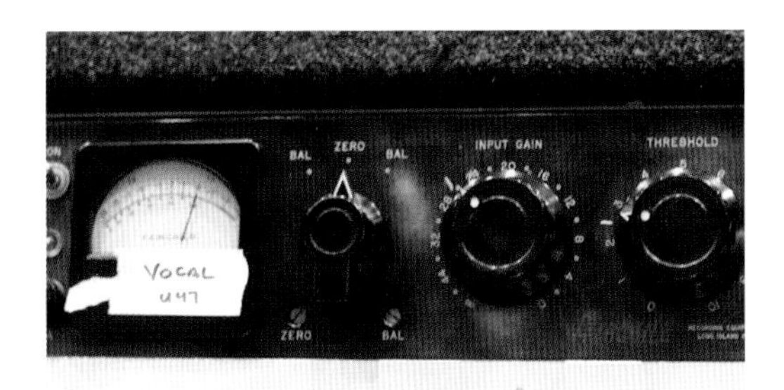

Fairchild 660 (mono) and 670 (stereo)

Al's Preferred Application. Vocals

A Note from Al. I wish I owned a Fairchild. They're hard to get, and they go for about $35,000. Capitol has one and I use it all the time on vocals. Some things are just magical. If you have a U 47 hooked up to the Fairchild 660, there's just a magic to that's real.

People will bring me something to mix and I'll run the vocal through the Fairchild and they'll say, "Oh my God! What did you do?" There's a quality that the 660 has that's just amazing. I set it up the same way I do for bass, where I just tap the gain reduction by one or two dB. I just run it through for the warmth of the sound. I'm not looking for gain reduction.

Technical Data

Input impedance	600 ohms
Output impedance	600 ohms
Range of input level	0 dBm to +16 dBm. (-4 dBm to +16 dBm) (model 660)
Output level	+4 or +8 dBm (+27 dBm clipping point)
Gain	7dB (16dB Model 660)
Frequency response	20 cycles to 15 kc +/- 1dB.
Separation	A-B position: 60 dB vertical-lateral position: 40 dB (does not apply to 660)
Noise level	70 dB below +4 dBm
Limiting noises	Below audibility
Intermodulation or harmonic distortion	Less than 1% at any level up to + 18 dBm output (no limiting) Less than 1% at dB limiting +12 dBm output
Attack time	.2 milliseconds on positions 1, 2 and 6 .4 milliseconds on positions 3,4 and 5 (adjustable)
Release time	Position 1: .3 sec, Position 2: .8 seconds, Position 3: 2 seconds, Position 4: 5 seconds, Position 5: Automatic function of program material: 2 seconds for individual peaks. 10 seconds for multiple peaks. 25 seconds for consistently high program level.
Compression ratio	A function of the amount of limiting as well as setting of the two threshold controls which can be set to operate at ratios from 1:2 to 1:30
Power Requirements	115 volts, 50-60 cycles AC, 3 amps.
Stability	Unit maintains stability of gain, gain reduction and balance over the range of line voltage fluctuations from 100 to 127 volts.

Summit Audio Tube Leveling Amplifier TLA-100A compressors

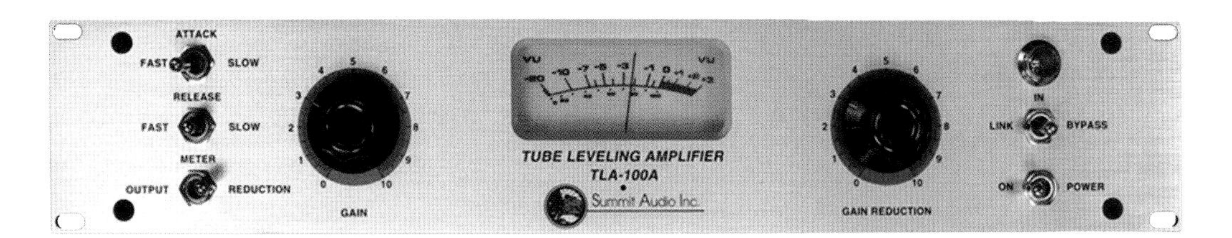

Summit Audio Tube Leveling Amplifier TLA-100A compressors

Al's Preferred Application. Upright bass

A Note from Al. I have two Summit TLA-100As and I use one for each of the two Neumann M 149s that I use on the upright bass. I just barely tap the level because I'm not looking for compression. Since the Summits are tube compressors, they have a personality to the sound that I really love. And it's hard to explain what the personality is. You really need to run the signal through it and let somebody hear it with it in, and then with it out. And they'll hear the difference. There's a richness and warmth to the sound—an added presence. The compressor is working just a dB or two, and I don't boost the output to make up for the compression. I just leave it at unity.

The TLA-100As are something that I use instead of a compressor like the Universal Audio 1176. For me, the 1176 is kind of noisy, but the Summits are very clean. I have a couple and Capitol has a couple, so there are always four around to use when I need them. I also don't use the LA-2A much. I might use it on a guitar now and again, but I prefer the Summits.

Technical Data

Max input level	+26dBu
Max output level (XLR)	+20dBu
Max gain	+34dBu
Frequency response	20Hz- 20kHz +/- 1dB with 5dB compression
Signal to noise ratio	124dB
Attack times	180uS-100mS
Release times	32mS- 1.5S
THD + Noise	0.09% @ 1kHz, 0dB out
Dynamic Range	60dB
Vacuum tubes	single 12AX7A

Conclusion

I obviously have developed my list of go-to microphones as a result of my experiences and my preferences, but there's no substitute for hearing what the different mics sound like, and then deciding what will work best on your music. Get together with friends or other engineers who have microphone collections, and try all of the mics on different things. You'll learn a lot that way, and it won't take long until you have your favorites.

Also, everybody finds his or her own way to work. I really like the bleed between mics. That's why I use a lot of omnidirectional microphones. I embrace leakage and bleed, but a lot of engineers don't want any bleed. It comes down to what are the best mics for the music you record. For me, I use great microphones on everything I do—the very best I can find—because I want the bleed between mics to support the sound. For my style, I need the leakage to sound great, too. If I used cheap microphones, the bleed would add a sound to my recordings that I wouldn't like—they wouldn't sound anything like the recordings I get with my mic choices. They wouldn't be warm- and smooth-sounding the way I like a recording to sound.

Even though I have a good list of mics that I like to use for certain things, I'm always experimenting with new microphones. Every time something new comes out, I want to try it as soon as I can get my hands on it.

I want the very best sound I can get for everything I record. That's important. I don't use plug-ins. Somebody was telling me about how great the Fairchild plug-in was, but my response is, "Have you ever heard the difference between a Fairchild plug-in and a real Fairchild?" If you make that comparison, you'll understand why I don't use plug-ins. Plug-ins are great for guys mixing in the box, and that's all they have, but I mix on a large console, and I have all the original stuff. I don't know of any plug-in that sounds as good as the original piece of equipment. I have engineers who will stop by a session, and they can't believe how good everything sounds without any EQ or compression.

When I teach at Mix With The Masters, I challenge the students to give me their mix of a tune where they use all the plug-ins, and EQ, and compression they want. Then they'll let me mix it from their hard drive without any EQ or compression, and just a little bit of echo. Their jaws drop down to their chest! They can't believe I can make it sound that good without a bunch of EQ and compression. But really, what's happening when you add so much processing is that the phasing is going all over the place, and that's what's causing the problems with their mixes. It's hard for me to listen to that kind of stuff. It just doesn't sound natural to me. When Niko Bolas was at Capitol up on the second floor, he had me mix something in the box up in his room, and then I went down to Studio C and mixed the same thing, and it just sound so much better. I couldn't believe it. That was it for me. Although, Niko played me something he'd been working on all in the box and it sounded amazing. It had depth and it was great. You can get great mixes in the box if you know what you're doing.

I'm really proud when I see some of the people who I've helped in these classes doing really great work. I like helping people raise the level of their work. When we started the METAlliance group with the seven of us, at the time, it was about giving something like the Good Housekeeping Seal of Approval to equipment. It was about being able to say we had all listened closely to this piece of gear and thought it was really a quality product that you could trust. So it's about helping people do a better job with the right tools. We just did a seminar in New York, and 40 people came, and many of them said it was life-changing because they could see how we work, and even though we all work differently, they can still learn a little something from each one of us. That's what it's all about. We've never made any money off the METAlliance. It's all about giving back. That's why we all invest our time.

About the Author

Al Schmitt has worked with the best and the brightest in the recording industry, including Frank Sinatra, Barbra Streisand, Neil Young, Bob Dylan, Usher, and Dr. Dre, to name a few. He has recorded and mixed over 150 gold and platinum records and has gone on to receive 23 Grammys for engineering albums by such artists as Steely Dan, Toto, Natalie Cole, Quincy Jones, Diana Krall, Luis Miguel, Ray Charles, Chick Corea, DeeDee Bridgewater, and Paul McCartney.

Schmitt was inducted into the TEC Awards Hall of Fame in 1997, and he was awarded the NARAS Award for Lifetime Achievement in 2006. In 2015, he received a star on the Hollywood Walk of Fame in front of the Capitol Records building—the first engineer to be so honored.